Christianity Unveiled;

BEING

AN EXAMINATION

OF

THE PRINCIPLES AND EFFECTS

OF THE

Christian Religion

=========

TRANSLATED FROM THE FRENCH OF BOULANGER

BY W. M. JOHNSON.

=========

1819

A
LETTER
FROM
THE AUTHOR TO A FRIEND

I RECEIVE, Sir, with gratitude, the remarks which you send me upon my work. If I am sensible to the praises you condescend to give it, I am too fond of truth to be displeased with the frankness with which you propose your objections. I find them sufficiently weighty to merit all my attention. He but ill deserves the title of philosopher, who has not the courage to hear his opinions contradicted. We are not divines; our disputes are of a nature to terminate amicably; they in no way resemble those of the apostles of superstition, who endeavour to overreach each other by captious arguments, and who, at the expence of good faith, contend only to advocate the cause of their vanity and their prejudices. We both desire the happiness of mankind, we both search after truth; this being the case, we cannot disagree.

You begin by admitting the necessity of examining religion, and submitting opinions to the decision of reason. You acknowledge that Christianity cannot sustain this trial, and that in the eye of good sense it can never appear to be any thing but a tissue of absurdities, of unconnected fables, senseless dogmas, puerile ceremonies, and notions borrowed from the Chaldeans, Egyptians, Phenicians, Grecians, and Romans. In one word, you confess that this religious system is only the deformed offspring of almost all ancient superstitions, begotten by oriental fanaticism, and diversely modified by the circumstances and prejudices of those who have since pretended to be the inspired ambassadors of God, and the interpreters of his will.

You tremble at the horrors which the intolerant spirit of Christians has caused them to commit, whenever they had power to do it; you feel that a religion founded on a sanguinary deity must be a religion of blood. You lament that phrenzy, which in infancy takes possession of princes and people, and renders them equally the slaves of superstition and her priests; which prevents their acquaintance with their true interests, renders them deaf to reason, and turns them aside from the great objects by which they ought to be occupied. You confess that a religion founded upon enthusiasm or imposture can have no sure principles; that it must prove an eternal source of disputes, and always end in causing troubles, persecutions, and ravages; especially when political power conceives itself indispensably obliged to enter into its quarrels. In fine, you go so far as to agree that a good Christian who follows literally the conduct prescribed to him as the most perfect by the gospel, knows not in this world any thing of those duties on which true morality is founded; and that if he wants energy he must prove an useless misanthrope, or if his temper be warm, a turbulent fanatic.

After acknowledging all this, how could it happen that you should pronounce any work a dangerous one! You tell me that a wise man ought to think only for himself; that to the populace a religion is necessary, be it good or bad; that it is a restraint necessary to gross and ignorant minds, which, without it, would have no longer any motive for abstaining from vice. You look upon a reform of religious prejudices as impossible, because it is the interest of many of those persons who alone can effect it, to continue mankind in that ignorance of which themselves reap the advantage. These, if I mistake not, are the weightiest of your objections. I will endeavour to remove them.

Books are generally written for that part of a nation whose circumstances, education, and sentiments, place them above the commission of crimes. This enlightened portion of society, which governs the other, reads and judges of writings; if they contain maxims false or injurious, they are soon either condemned to oblivion, or held up to public execration; if they contain only truth, they are not in danger. Fanatics and ignorant people are the disturbers of society. Sensible, enlightened, and disinterested persons are ever the friends of peace.

You are not, Sir, of the number of pusillanimous thinkers, who believe that truth is capable of doing harm. It does to those only who deceive mankind, and to the rest the human species it will always be useful. You ought to have been convinced that the evils with which mankind are afflicted, arise only from our errors, our prejudices, our interests misunderstood, and the false ideas we attach objects.

In fine, it is easy to see that the policy and morality, of man have been particularly corrupted by their religious prejudices. Was it not religious and supernatural ideas which caused sovereigns to be looked upon as gods? It is then religion which raised up tyrants and despots; tyrants and despots make wicked laws; their example corrupted the the great, the great corrupted the lower classes of mankind; these vitiated beings became unhappy slaves, employed either in injuring themselves, flattering the great; or struggling to get clear of their misery. Kings were styled images of God: they were absolute like him; they created justice and injustice; their wills often sanctified oppression, violence, and rapine. The means of obtaining their favours were vice and meanness. Thus nations became filled with perverted citizens, who, under leaders corrupted by religious notions made continually a war, either open or clandestine, and were left destitute of any motive for practising virtue.

Has this religion influenced the manners of sovereigns, who derive their divine power from it? Do we not behold princes, overflowing with faith, continually undertaking the most unjust wars; wasting the blood and treasure of their subjects; wrenching the bread from the hands of the poor; permitting and even commanding every species of injustice? Does this religion, considered by so many sovereigns as the support of their thrones, render them more humane, temperate, chaste, or faithful to their oaths? Alas! when we consult history, we there find sovereigns who were orthodox, zealous, and religious to a scruple, and at the same time guilty of perjury, usurpation, adultery, robbery, and murder; men who, in fine, behaved as if they feared not the God whom they honoured with their mouths. Among the courtiers who surrounded them, we see a continual alliance of Christianity and vice, devotion and iniquity, religion and treason. Among the priests of a poor and crucified God, who found their existence upon religion, and pretend that without it there could be no morality, do we not see reigning amongst them, pride, avarice, wantonness, and revenge?

Amongst us, education is very little attended to by the government, which shews the most profound indifference concerning an object the most essential to the happiness of states. With most modern nations public education is confined to the teaching languages, useless to most who learn them. Christians, instead of morality, inculcate the marvellous fables and incomprehensible dogmas of a religion extremely repugnant to right reason. At the first step a young man makes in his studies, he is taught that he ought to renounce the testimony of his senses, to reject his reason as an unfaithful guide, and blindly conform himself to the dictates of his masters. But who are these masters? Priests, whose interest it is to continue mankind in errors, of which they alone reap the advantage. Can the abject and isolated mind of these mercenary pedagogues be capable of instructing their pupils in that of which themselves are ignorant? Will they teach them to love the public good, to serve their try, to know the duties of the man and citizen? Certainly not; we can expect nothing from the bands of such teachers but ignorant and superstitious pupils, who, if they have profited of the lessons they have received, are unacquainted with every thing necessary in society, of which they must consequently become useless members.

On whatever side we cast our eyes, we see the study of the objects most important to man totally neglected. Morality, in which I also comprehend policy, is considered of very little importance in European education. The only morality taught by Christians is, the enthusiastic, impracticable, contradictory, and uncertain morality contained in the gospel. This is calculated only to degrade the mind, to render virtue odious, to form abject slaves, and break the Spring of the soul; or, if it is sown in warm and active minds, to produce turbulent fanatics, capable of shaking the foundations of society.

Notwithstanding the inutility and perversity of the morality which Christianity teaches mankind, its partisans presume to tell us that without this religion we cannot have morals. But what is it to have morals, in the language of Christians? It is to pray without ceasing, to frequent churches, to do penance, and to abstain from pleasure; it is to live in selfishness and solitude. What good results to society from these practices, all of which may be observed by a man, who has not the shadow of virtue? If such morals lead to heaven, they are very useless on earth. But certain it is, that a man may be a faithful observer of all that Christianity enjoins, without possessing any of the virtues which reason shews to be necessary to the support of political society.

It is necessary, then, to carefully distinguish *Christian* morality from *political* morality; the former makes saints, the latter citizens: one makes men useless, or even hurtful to the world; the other has for its object the formation of members useful to society; men active and vigorous, who are capable of serving it, who fulfil the duties of husbands, fathers, friends, and companions, whatever may be their metaphysical opinions, which, let Theologists say what they will, are much less sure than the invariable rules of good sense.

In fact, it is certain, that man is a social being, who in all things seeks his own happiness, that he does good when he finds it his interest; that he is not commonly bad, because that would be contrary to his welfare. This being premised let education teach men to know the relations which exist among themselves, and the arising from those relations; let governments calling to their aid laws, rewards and punishments, confirm the lessons given by education; let happiness accompany useful and virtuous actions, let shame, contempt, and chastisement be the rewards of vice. Then would mankind have a true morality, founded in their own nature upon their mutual and the interest of nations at large. This morality, independent of the sub. lime notions of Theology, perhap's have very little in common with Christian morality; but society has nothing to lose from this circumstance, as has already been proved.

When the people receive a proper education, which, by inspiring them early in life with virtuous principles, will habituate them to do homage to virtue, detest crimes, contemn vice, and shrink from infamy; such an education cannot be vain, when continual example shall prove to the citizens that talents and virtue are the only means of arriving at honour, fortune, distinction, consideration, and favour; and that vice conducts only to contempt and ignominy.

If the clergy have usurped from the sovereign power the right of instructing the people, let the latter reassume its rights, or at least not suffer the former to enjoy the exclusive liberty of governing the manners of mankind, and dictating their morality. Let them teach if they please, that their God transforms himself into bread, but let them never teach that we ought to hate or destroy those who refuse to believe this ineffable mystery. Let no individual in society have the power of exciting citizens to rebellion, of sowing discord, breaking the hands which unite the people amongst one another, and disturbing the public tranquillity for the sake of opinions. If it be said that all governments think it their interest to support religious prejudices, and manage the clergy through policy, although they themselves are undeceived; I answer, that it is easy to convince every enlightened government, that it is their true interest to govern a happy people; that upon the happiness it procures the nation, depends the stability and safety of the government; in one word, that a nation composed of wise and virtuous citizens, are much more powerful than a troop of ignorant and corrupted slaves, whom the government is forced to deceive in order to satisfy, and to deluge with impositions that it may succeed in any enterprise.

Thus let us not despair, that truth will one day force its way even to thrones. If the light of reason and science reaches princes with so much difficulty, it is because interested priests and starveling courtiers endeavour to keep them in a perpetual infancy, point out to them chimerical prospects of power and grandeur, and thus turn away their attention from objects necessary to their true happiness.

Every government must feel that their power will always be tottering and precarious, so long as it depends for support on the phantoms of religion, the errors of the people, and the caprices of the priesthood. It must feel the inconveniences resulting from fanatic administration, which have hitherto produced nothing but ignorance and presumption, nothing but obstinate, weak citizens, incapable of doing service to the state, and ready to receive the false impressions of guides who would lead them astray. It must perceive what immense resources might be derived from the wealth which has been accumulated by a body of useless men, who, under pretensions of teaching the nation, cheat and devour it. [Footnote: Some have thought that the clergy might one day serve as a barrier against despotism, but experience sufficiently proves that this body always stipulates for itself alone.] Upon this foundation (which to the shame of mankind be it said, has hitherto served only to support sacerdotal pride) a wise government might raise establishments which would become useful to the state in forming the youth, cherishing talents, rewarding virtuous services, and comforting the people.

I flatter myself, Sir, that these reflections will exculpate me in your eyes. I do not hope for the suffrages of those who feel themselves interested in the continuance of the evils suffered by their fellow-citizens; it in not such whom I aim to convince; nothing can be made to appear evident to vicious and unreasonable men. But I presume to hope, that you will cease to look upon my book as dangerous, and my expectations as altogether chimerical. Many immoral men have attacked the Christian religion, because it opposed their propensities; many wise men have despised it, because to them it appeared ridiculous; many persons have looked upon it with indifference, because they did not feel its real inconveniences. I attack it as a citizen, because it appears to me to be injurious to the welfare of the state, an enemy to the progress of the human mind, and opposed to the principles of true morality, from which political interests can never be separated. It remains only for me to say, with a poet, who was, like myself, an enemy to superstition:

....

Si tibi vera videtur,

Dede manus, et si falsa est, accingere contra.

I am, &c.

Christianity Unveiled.

=========

CHAP. I.

INTRODUCTION.

OF THE NECESSITY OF AN INQUIRY RESPECTING RELIGION, AND THE OBSTACLES WHICH ARE MET IN PURSUING THIS INQUIRY.

 A REASONABLE being ought in all his actions to aim at his own happiness and that of his fellow-creatures. Religion, which is held up as an object most important to our temporal and eternal felicity, can be advantageous to us only so far as it renders our existence happy in *this world*, or as we are assured that it will fulfil the flattering promises which it makes us respecting another.--Our duty towards God, whom we look upon as the ruler of our destinies, can be founded, it is said, not only on the evils which we fear on his part. It is then necessary that man should examine the grounds of his fears. He ought, for this purpose, to consult experience and reason, which are the only guides to truth. By the benefits which he derives from religion in the visible world which he inhabits, he may judge of the reality of those blessings for which it leads him to hope in that invisible world, to which it commands him to turn his views.

 Mankind, for the most part, hold to their religion through habit. They have never seriously examined the reasons why they are attached to it, the motives of their conduct, or the foundations of their opinions. Thus, what has ever been considered as most important to all, has been of all things least subjected to scrutiny. Men blindly follow on in the paths which their fathers trod; they believe, because in infancy they were told they must believe; they, hope, because their progenitors hoped, and they tremble, because they trembled. Scarcely ever have they deigned to render an account of the motives of their belief. Very few men have leisure to examine, or fortitude to analyze, the objects of their habitual veneration, their blind attachment, or their traditional fears. Nations are carried away in the torrent of habit, example, and prejudice. Education habituates the mind to opinions the most monstrous, as it accustoms the body to attitudes the most uneasy. All that has long existed appears sacred to the eyes of man; they think it sacrilege to examine things stamped with the seal of antiquity. Prepossessed in favour of the wisdom of their fathers, they have not the presumption to investigate what has received their sanction. They see not that man has ever been the dupe of his prejudices, his hopes, and his fears; and that the same reasons have almost always rendered this enquiry equally impracticable.

The vulgar, busied in the labours necessary to their subsistence, place a blind confidence in those who pretend to guide them, give up to them the right of thinking, and submit without murmuring to all they prescribe. They believe they shall offend God, if they doubt for a moment, the veracity of those who speak to them in his name. The great, the rich, the men of the world, even when they are more enlightened than the vulgar, have found it their interest to conform to received prejudices, and even to maintain them; or, swallowed up in dissipation, pleasure, and effeminacy, they have no time to bestow on a religion, which they easily accommodate to their passions, propensities, and fondness for amusement. In childhood, we receive all the impressions others wish to make upon us; we have neither the capacity, experience, or courage, necessary to examine what is taught us by those, on whom our weakness renders us dependent. In youth, the ardour of our passions, and the continual ebriety of our senses, prevent our thinking seriously of a religion, too austere and gloomy to please; if by chance a young man examines it, he does it with partiality, or without perseverance; he is often disgusted with a single glance of the eye on an object so disgusting. In riper age, new passions and cares, ideas of ambition, greatness, power, the desire of riches, and the hurry of business, absorb the whole attention of man, or leave him but few moments to think of religion, which he never has the leisure to scrutinize. In old age, the faculties are blunted, habits become incorporated with the machine, and the senses are debilitated by time and infirmity; and we are no longer able to penetrate back to the source of our opinions; besides, the fear of death then renders an examination, over which terror commonly presides, very liable to suspicion.

Thus, religious opinions, once received, maintain their ground, through a long succession of ages; thus nations transmit from generation to generation ideas which they have never examined; they imagine their welfare to be attached to institutions in which, were the truth known, they would behold the source of the greater part of their misfortunes. Civil authority also flies to the support of the prejudices of mankind, compels them to ignorance by forbidding inquiry, and holds itself in continual readiness to punish all who attempt to undeceive themselves.

Let us not be surprised, then, if we see error almost inextricably interwoven with human nature. All things seem to concur to perpetuate our blindness, and hide the truth from us. Tyrants detest and oppress truth, because it dares to dispute their unjust and chimerical titles; it is opposed by the priesthood because it annihilates their superstitions. Ignorance, indolence, and passion render the great part of mankind accomplices of those who strive to deceive them, in order to keep their necks beneath the yoke, and profit by their miseries. Hence nations groan under hereditary evils, thoughtless of a remedy; being either ignorant of the cause, or so long accustomed to disease, that they have lost even the desire of health.

If religion be the object most important to mankind, if it extends its influences not only over our conduct in this life, but also over our eternal happiness, nothing, can demand from us a more serious examination. Yet it is of all things, that, respecting which, mankind exercise the most implicit credulity. The same man, who examines with scrupulous nicety things of little moment to his welfare, wholly neglects inquiry concerning the motives, which determine him to believe and perform things, on which, according to his own confession, depend both his temporal and eternal felicity. He blindly abandons himself to those whom chance has given him for guides; he confides to them the care of thinking for him, and even makes a merit of his own indolence and credulity. In matters of religion, infancy and barbarity seem to be the boast of the greater part of the human race.

Nevertheless, men have in all ages appeared. who, shaking off the prejudices of their fellows, have dared to lift before their eyes the light of truth. But what could their feeble voice effect, against errors imbibed at the breast, confirmed by habit, authorised by example, and fortified by a policy, which often became the accomplice of its own ruin? The stentorian clamours of imposture soon overwhelm the calm exhortations of the advocates of reason. In vain shall the philosopher endeavour to inspire mankind with courage, so long as they tremble beneath the rod of priests and kings.

The surest means of deceiving mankind, and perpetuating their errors, is to deceive them in infancy. Amongst many nations at the present day, education seems designed only to form fanatics, devotees, and monks; that is to say, men either useless or injurious to society. Few are the places in which it is calculated to form good citizens. Princes, to whom a great part of the earth is at present unhappily subjected, are commonly the victims of a superstitious education, and remain all their lives in the profoundest ignorance of their own duties, and the truest interests of the states which they govern. Religion seems to have been invented only to render both kings and people equally the slaves of the priesthood. The latter is continually busied in raising obstacles to the felicity of nations. Wherever this reigns, other governments have but a precarious power; and citizens become indolent, ignorant, destitute of greatness of soul, and, in short, of every quality necessary to the happiness of society.

If, in a state where the Christian religion is professed, we find some activity, some science, and an approach to social manners; it is, because nature, whenever it is in her power, restores mankind to reason, and obliges them to labour for their own felicity. Were all Christian nations exactly conformed to their principles, they must be plunged into the most profound inactivity. Our countries would be inhabited by a small number of pious savages, who would meet only to destroy each other. For, why should a man mingle with the affairs of a world, which his religion informs him is only a place of passage? What can be the industry of that people, who believe themselves commanded by their God to live in continual fear, to pray, to groan, and afflict themselves incessantly? How can a society exist which is composed of men who are convinced that, in their zeal for religion, they ought to hate and destroy all, whose opinions differ from their own ? How can we expect to find humanity, justice, or any virtue, amongst a horde of fanatics, who copy in their conduct, a cruel, dissembling, and dishonest God? A God who delights in the tears of his unhappy creatures, who sets for them the ambush, and then punishes them for having fallen into it! A God who himself ordains robbery, persecution, and carnage!

Such, however, are the traits with which the Christian religion represents the God which it has inherited from the Jews. This God was a sultan, a despot, a tyrant, to whom all things were lawful. Yet he is held up to us as a model of perfection. Crimes, at which human nature revolts, have been committed in his name; and the greatest villainies have been justified by the pretence of their being committed, either by his command, or to merit his favour. Thus the Christian religion, which boasts of being the only true support of morality, and of furnishing mankind with the strongest motives for the practice of virtue, has proved to them a source of divisions, oppressions, and the blackest crimes. Under the pretext of bringing peace on earth, it has overwhelmed it with hate, discord, and war. It furnishes the human race with a thousand ingenious means of tormenting themselves, and scatters amongst them scourges unknown before.

The Christian, possessed of common sense, must bitterly regret the tranquil ignorance of his idolatrous ancestors.

If the manners of nations have gained nothing by the Christian religion, governments of which it has pretended to be the support, have drawn from it advantages equally small. It establishes to itself in every state a separate power, and becomes the tyrant or the enemy of every other power. Kings were always the slaves of priests; or if they refused to bow the knee, they were proscribed, stripped of their privileges, and exterminated either by subjects whom religion had excited to revolt, or assassins whose hands she had armed with her sacred poignard. Before the introduction of the Christian religion, those who governed the state commonly governed the priesthood; since that period, sovereigns have dwindled into the first slaves of the priesthood, the mere executors of its vengeance and its decrees.

Let us then conclude, that the Christian religion has no right to boast of procuring advantages either to policy or morality. Let us tear aside the veil with which it envelopes itself. Let us penetrate back to its source. Let us pursue it in its course; we shall find that, founded on imposture, ignorance, and credulity, it can never be useful but to men who wish to deceive their fellow-creatures. We shall find, that it will never cease to generate the greatest evils among mankind, and that instead of producing the felicity it promises, it is formed to cover the earth with outrages, and deluge it in blood; that it will plunge the human race in delerium and vice, and blind their eyes to their truest interests and their plainest duties.

CHAP. II.

SKETCH OF THE HISTORY OF THE JEWS.

IN a small country, almost unknown to others, lived a nation, the founders of which having long been slaves among the Egyptians, were delivered from their servitude by a priest of Heliopolis, who, by means of his superior genius and knowledge, gained the ascendancy over them.[1] This man, known by the name of Moses, being educated in the mysteries of a religion, which was fertile in prodigies, and the mother of superstitions, placed himself at the head of a band of fugitives, whom he persuaded that he was an interpreter of the will of their God, whose immediate commands he pretended to receive. He proved his mission, it is said, by works which appeared supernatural to men ignorant of the operations of nature, and the resources of art. The first command that he gave them on the part of his God was to rob their masters, whom they about to desert. When he had thus enriched them with the spoils of Egypt, being sure of their confidence, he conducted them into a desert, where, during forty

---

[1] Maneton and Cheremon, Egyptian historians, respecting whom testimonies have been transmitted to us by Joseph[us] the Jew, inform us that a multitude of lepers were drawn out of Egypt by king Amenophis; and that these exiles elected for their leader a priest of Heliopolis whose name was Moses, and who formed for them a religion and a code of laws. *Joseph contre Appion.* liv. i. chap. 9, 11,12.

Diodorus Siculus also relates the history of Moses. Vide translation of Abbe Terrasson.

Be this as it may, Moses, by the confession of the Bible itself, began his career by assassinating an Egyptian, who was quarrelling with an Hebrew; after which he fled into Arabia, and married the daughter of an idolatrous priest, by whom be was often reproached for his cruelty. Thence he returned into Egypt, and placed himself at the head of his nation, which was dissatisfed with king Pharaoh. Moses reigned very tyrannically; the examples of Korah, Dathau, and Abiram, prove to what kind of people he had an aversion. He at last disappeared like Romulus, no one being able to find his body, or the place of his sepulture.

years, he accustomed them to the blindest obedience. He taught them the will of heaven, the marvellous fables of their forefathers, and the ridiculous ceremonies to which he pretended the Most High attached his favours. He was particularly careful to inspire them with the most envenomed. hatred against the gods of other nations, and the most refined cruelty to those who adored them. By means of carnage and severity, he rendered them a nation of slaves, obsequious to his will, ready to second his passions, and sacrifice themselves to gratify his ambitious views. In one word, he made the Hebrews monsters of phrenzy and ferocity. After having thus animated them with the spirit of destruction, he showed them the lands and possessions of their neighbours, as an inheritance assigned them by God himself.

Proud of the protection of Jehovah, the Hebrews marched forth to victory. Heaven authorised in them knavery and cruelty. Religion, united to avidity, rendered them deaf to the cries of nature; and, under the conduct of inhuman chiefs, they destroyed the Canaanitish nations with a barbarity, at which every man must revolt, whose reason is not wholly annihilated by superstition. Their fury destroyed every thing, even infants at the breast, in those cities whether these monsters carried their victorious arms. By the commands of their God, or his prophets, good faith was violated, justice outraged, and cruelty exercised.

This nation of robbers, usurpers, and murderers, at length established themselves in a country, not indeed very fertile, but with which they found delicious in comparison with the desert in which they had so long wandered. Here, under the authority of the visible priests of their hidden God, they founded a state, detestable to its neighbours, and at all times the object of their contempt or their hatred. The priesthood, under the title of a Theocracy, for a long time governed this blind and ferocious people. They were persuaded that in obeying their priests they obeyed God himself.

Notwithstanding their superstition, the Hebrews at length, forced by circumstances, or perhaps weary of the yoke of priesthood, determined to have a king, according to the example of other nations. But in the choice of their monarch they thought themselves obliged to have recourse to a prophet. Thus began the monarchy of the Hebrews. Their princes, however, were always crossed in their enterprises, by inspired priests and ambitious prophets, who continually laid obstacles in the way of every sovereign whom they did not find sufficiently submissive to their own wills. The history of the Jews at all times shows us nothing but kings blindly obedient to the priesthood, or at war with it, and perishing under its blows.

The ferocious and ridiculous superstitions of the Jews rendered them at once the natural enemies of mankind, and the object of their contempt. They were always treated with great severity by those who made inroads upon their territory. Successively enslaved slaved by the Egyptians, the Babylonians, and the Grecians, they experienced from their masters the bitterest treatment, which was indeed but too well deserved. Often disobedient to their God, whose own cruelty, as well as the tyranny of his priests, frequently disgusted them, they were never faithful to their princes. In vain were they crushed beneath sceptres of iron; it was impossible to render them loyal subjects. The Jews were always the dupes of their prophets, and in their greatest distresses, their obstinate fanaticism, ridiculous hopes, and indefatigable credulity, supported them against the blows of fortune. At last, conquered with the rest of the earth, Judea submitted to the Roman yoke.

Despised by their new masters, the Jews were treated hardly, and with great haughtiness ; for their laws, as well as their conduct, had inspired the hearts of their conquerors with the liveliest detestation. Soured by misfortune, they became more blind, fanatic, and seditious. Exalted by the pretended promises of their God; full of confidence in oracles, which have always announced to them a felicity which they have never tasted; encouraged by enthusiasts, or by impostors, who successively profit by their credulity; the Jews have, to this day, expected the coming of a *Messiah*, a monarch, a deliverer, who shall free them from the yokes beneath which they groan, and cause their nation to reign over all other nations in the universe.

CHAP. III.

SKETCH OF THE HISTORY OF THE CHRISTIAN RELIGION.

In the midst of this nation, thus disposed to feed on hope and chimera, a new prophet arose, whose sectaries in process of time have changed the face of the earth. A poor Jew, who pretended to be descended from the royal at house of David,[2] after being long unknown in his own country, emerges from obscurity, and goes forth to make proselytes. He succeeded amongst some of the most ignorant part of the populace. To them he preached his doctrines, and taught them that he was the Son or God, the deliverer of his oppressed nation, and the Messiah announced by the prophets. His disciples, being either impostors, or themselves deceived, rendered a clamorous testimony of his power, and declared that his mission had been proved by miracles without number. The only prodigy which he was incapable of effecting, was that of convincing the Jews, who, far from being touched with his beneficent and marvellous works, caused him to suffer an ignominious death. Thus the Son of God died in the sight of all Jerusalem; but his followers declare that he was secretly resuscitated three days after his death. Visible to them alone, and invisible to the nation which he came to enlighten and convert to his doctrine, Jesus, after his resurrection, say they, conversed some time with his disciples, and then ascended into heaven, where, having again become equal to God the Father, he shares with him the adorations and homages of the sectaries of his law. These sectaries, by accumulating superstitions,

---

[2] The Jews say that Jesus was the son of one Pandira, or Panther, who had seduced his mother Mary, a milliner, the wife of Jochanan. According to others, Pandira, by some artifice, enjoyed her several times while she thought him her husband; after which, she becoming pregnant, her husband, suspicious of her fidelity, retired into Babylon. Some say that Jesus was taught magic in Egypt, from whence he went and exercised his art in Galilee, where he was put to death. --Vide Peiffer, *Theol. Jud. and Mahom. &c. Principia. Lypsiae, 1687.*

inventing impostures, and fabricating dogmas and mysteries, have, by little and little, heaped up a distorted and unconnected system of religion which is called *Christianity*, after the name of Christ its founder.

The different nations, to which the Jews were successively subjected, had infected them with a multitude of Pagan dogmas. Thus the Jewish religion. Egyptian in its origin, adopted many of the rites and opinions of the people, with whom the Jews conversed. We need not then be surprised, if we see the Jews, and the Christians their successors, filled with notions borrowed of the Phenicians, the Magi or Persians, the Greeks and the Romans. The errors of mankind respecting religion have a general resemblance; they appear to differ only by their combinations. The commerce of the Jews and Christians with the Grecians, made them acquainted with the philosophy of Plato, so analogous to the romantic spirit of the orientals, and so conformable to the genius of a religion which boasts in being inaccessible to reason. [3]Paul, the most ambitious and enthusiastic of the apostles, carried his doctrines, seasoned with the sublime and marvellous, among the people of Greece and Asia, and even the inhabitants of Rome. He gained proselytes, as every man who addresses himself to the imagination of ignorant people may do; and he may be justly styled the principal founder of a religion, which, without him, could never have spread far; for the rest of its followers were ignorant men, from whom he soon separated himself to become the leader of his own sect. [4]

The conquests of the Christian religion were, in its infancy, generally limited to the vulgar and ignorant. It was embraced only

---

[3] Origen says, that Celsus reproached Christ with having borrowed many of his maxims from Plato. See Origen contra Cel. chap. i. 6. Augustine confesses, that he found the beginning of the Gospel of John, in Plato; see S. Aug. Conf. I. vii. ch. 9, 10, 11. The notion of the word is evidently taken from Plato; the church has since found means of transplanting a great part of Plato, as we shall hereafter prove.

[4] The Ebionites, or first Christians, looked upon Saint Paul as in apostate and an heretic, because he wholly rejected the law of Moses, which the other apostles wished only to reform.

by the most abject amongst the Jews and Pagans. It is over men of this description that the marvellous has the greatest influence.⁵ An unfortunate God, the innocent victim of wickedness and cruelty, and an enemy to riches and the great, must have been an object of consolation to the wretched. The austerity, contempt of riches, and apparently disinterested cares of the first preachers of the gospel, whose ambition was limited to the government of *souls*; the equality of rank and property enjoined by their religion, and the mutual succours interchanged by its followers; these were objects well calculated to excite the desires of the poor, and multiply Christians. The union, concord, and reciprocal affection, recommended to the first Christians, must have been seductive to ingenious minds: their submissive temper, their patience in indigence, obscurity, and distress, caused their infant sect to be looked upon as little dangerous in a government accustomed to tolerate all sects. Thus, the founders of Christianity had many adherents among the *people* (*Le peuple*), and their opposers and enemies consisted chiefly of some idolatrous priests and Jews, whose interest it was to support the religion previously established. By little and little, this new system, covered with the clouds of mystery, took deep root, and became too strong and extensive to be suppressed. The Roman government saw too late the progress of an association it had despised. The Christians now become numerous, dared to brave the Pagan gods, even in their temples. The emperors and magistrates, disquieted at such proceedings, endeavoured to extinguish the sect which gave them umbrage. They persecuted such as they could not reclaim by milder means, and whom their fanaticism had rendered obstinate. The feelings of mankind are ever interested in favour of distress;

---

⁵ The first Christians were, by way of contempt, called Ebionites, which signifies beggars or mendicants. See Origen contra Celsum, lib. ii. and Euseb. Hist. Eccles. lib. iii. c. 37. Ebion, in Hebrew, signifies poor. The word Ebion has since been personified into the meaning of an heretic or the leader of a sect, who were excluded from sacred things, and scarcely considered as men. It promised them that they should one day have their turn, and that, in the other life, they should be happier than their masters.

and this persecution only served to increase the number of the friends of the Christians. The fortitude and constancy with which they suffered torment, appeared supernatural and divine in the eyes of those who were witnesses to it; their enthusiasm communicated itself, and produced new advocates for the sect, whew destruction was attempted.

After this explanation, let Christians no longer boast the marvelous progress of their religion. It was the religion of poverty; it announced a God who was poor. It was preached by the poor, to the poor sand ignorant. It gave them consolation in their misery. Even its gloomy ideas were analogous to the disposition of indigent and unhappy men. The union and concord so much admired in the earlier Christians, is by no means surprising. An infant and oppressed sect naturally remain united, and dread a separation of interests. It is astonishing that, in those early days, men who were themselves persecuted and treated as malcontents, should presume to preach intolerance and persecution. The tyranny exercised against them wrought no change in their sentiments. Tyranny only irritates the human mind, which is always invincible, when those opinions are attacked to which it has attached its welfare. Such is the inevitable effect of persecution. Yet Christians, who ought to be undeceived by the example of their own sect, have to this day been incapable of divesting themselves of the fury of persecution.

The Roman emperors, having themselves become Christians, that is to say, carried away by a general torrent, which obliged them to avail themselves of the support of a powerful sect, seated religion on the throne. They protected the church and its ministers, and endeavoured to inspire their courtiers with their own ideas. They beheld with a jealous eye those who retained their attachment to the ancient religion. They, at length, interdicted the exercise of it, and finished by forbidding it under the pain of death. They persecuted without measure those who held to the worship of their ancestors. The Christians now repaid the Pagans, with interest, the evils which they had before suffered from them. The Roman empire was shaken with convulsions, caused by the unbridled zeal of sovereigns and those *pacific* priests, who had just before preached nothing but mildness and toleration. The emperors, either from policy or superstition, loaded the priesthood with gifts and benefactions, which indeed were seldom repaid with gratitude. They established the authority of the latter; at length respected as divine what they had themselves created. Priests were relieved from all civil functions, that nothing might divert their minds from their sacred ministry.[6] Thus the leaders of a once insignificant and oppressed sect became independent. Being at last more powerful than kings, they soon arrogated to themselves the right of commanding them. These priests of a God of peace, almost continually at variance with each other, communicated the fury of their passions to their followers; and mankind were astonished to behold quarrels and miseries engendered, under the *law of grace*, which they had never experienced under the peaceful reign of the Divinities, who had formerly shared without dispute the adoration or mortals.

Such was the progress of a superstition, innocent in its origin, but which, in its course, far from producing happiness among mankind, became a bone of contention, and a fruitful source of calamities.

Peace upon earth, and good will towards men.

Thus is the gospel announced, which has cost the human race more blood than all other religious of the earth taken collectively.

Love the Lord thy God with all thy strength, and thy neighbour as thyself.

This, according to the God and Legislator of the Christians, is the sum of their duties. Yet we see it is impossible for Christians to love that severe and capricious God whom they worship. On the other hand, we see them eternally busied in tormenting, persecuting, and destroying their neighbours and brethren.

---

[6] See Tillemont's Life of Constantine. Vol. iv. Art. 32.

To find an explanation of these contradictions, it is sufficient to cast our eyes upon the God which the Christians inherited from the Jews. Not contented with the shocking colours in which he was painted, the Christians have still more disfigured his portrait. The Legislator of the Hebrews speaks only of the transient punishments of this life; the Christian represents his God as pouring out unbounded vengeance to all eternity. In one word, Christian fanaticism feeds itself with the idea of an hell, where its God, transformed into a ferocious executioner, as unjust as implacable, shall bathe himself in the tears of his wretched creatures, and perpetuate their existence, to render them eternally miserable. There, clothed in vengeance, he shall mock at the torments of sinners, and listen with rapture to the groans with which they shall make the brazen roofs of their prisons resound; not the smallest hope of some distant termination of their pains shall give them an interval of imaginary relief.

The Christians in adopting the terrible God of the Jews, have sublimed his cruelty. They represent him as the most capricious, wicked, and cruel tyrant which the human mind can conceive, and suppose him to treat his subjects with a barbarity and injustice truly worthy of a demon. In order to be convinced of this truth, let us contemplate, for a moment, a picture of the Jewish mythology, adopted and rendered still more extravagant by the Christians.

CHAP. IV.

OF THE CHRISTIAN MYTHOLOGY, OR THE IDEAS OF GOD, AND HIS CONDUCT, GIVEN US BY THE CHRISTIAN RELIGION.

GOD, by an inconceivable act of his omnipotence, created the universe out of nothing. [7]He made the earth for the residence of man, whom he created in his own image. Scarcely had this man, the prime object of the labours of his God, seem the light, when his Creator set a snare for him, into which he undoubtedly knew that he must fall. A serpent, who speaks, seduces a woman, who is not at all surprised at the phenomenon. She, being persuaded by the serpent, solicits her husband to eat of a fruit forbidden by God himself. Adam, the father of the human race, by this light fault, draws upon himself and his innocent posterity innumerable evils, which are followed, but not terminated by death. By the offence of only one man, the whole human race incurs the wrath of God, and they are at length punished for involuntary faults with an universal deluge. God repents having peopled the earth, and he finds it easier to drown and destroy the human race, than to change their hearts.

A small number of the just, however, escaped this destructive flood; but the deluged earth, and the destruction of mankind, did not satiate the implacable vengeance of their Creator. A new generation appeared. These, although descended from the friends of God, whom he had preserved in the general shipwreck of the world, incense him by new crimes. The almighty is represented as having been incapable of rendering his creature such as he desired him. A new torrent of corruption carries away mankind; and wrath is again excited in the bosom of Jehovah.

---

[7] Ex nihilo nihil fit, was considered as an axiom by ancient philosophers. The creation, as admitted by the Christians of the present day, that is to say, the eduction of all things from nothing, is a theological invention, not indeed, of very remote date. The word Barah, which is used in Genesis, signifies to compose, arrange, to dispose matter already existing.

Partial in his affections and his preferences, he, at length, casts his eyes on an idolatrous Assyrian. He enters into an alliance with this man, and covenants that his posterity shall be multiplied to the number of the stars of heaven, or the sands of the sea, and that they shall for ever enjoy the favour of God. To this chosen race he reveals his will; for them, unmindful of his justice, he destroys whole nations. Nevertheless, this favoured race is not the more happy or the more attached to their God. They fly to strange gods, from whom they seek succours, which are refused to them by their own. They frequently insult the God who is able to exterminate them. Sometimes he punishes, sometimes consoles them; one while he hates them without cause, and another caresses them with as little reason. At last, finding it impossible to reclaim this perverse people, for whom he continues to feel the warmest tenderness, he sends amongst them his own son. To this son they will not listen. What do I say? This beloved son, equal to God his father, is put to an ignominious death by his favourite nation. His father, at the same time, finds it impossible to save the human race, without the sacrifice of his own son. Thus an innocent God becomes the victim of a just God, by whom he is beloved. Both consent to this strange sacrifice, judged necessary by a God, who knows that it will be useless to an hardened nation, which nothing can reclaim. We should expect that the death of this God, being useless to Israel, must serve, at least, to expiate the sins of the rest of the human race. Notwithstanding the eternal alliance with the Hebrews, solemnly sworn to by the Most High, and so many times renewed, that favourite nation find themselves at last deserted by their God, who could not reduce them to obedience. The merits of the sufferings and death of his Son, are applied to the nations before excluded from his bounty. These are reconciled to heaven, now become more just in regard to them, and return to grace. Yet, in spite of all the efforts of God, his favours are lavished in vain. Mankind continue to sin, enkindle the divine wrath, and render themselves worthy of the eternal punishments, previously prepared and destined for the greater part of the human race.

Such is the faithful history of the God, on whom the foundation of the Christian religion is laid. His conduct being so strange, cruel, and opposite to all reason, is it surprising to see the worshippers of this God ignorant of their duties, destitute of humanity and justice, and striving to assimilate themselves to the model of that barbarous divinity which they adore? What indulgence have mankind a right to expect from a God, who spared not even his own son? What indulgence can the Christian, who believes this fable, show to his fellow-creature? Ought he not to imagine that the surest means of pleasing his God, is to imitate his ferocity and cruelty? [8]

It is at least evident, that the sectaries of such a God must have a precarious morality, founded on principles destitute of all firmness. This God, in fact, is not always unjust and cruel; his conduct varies. Sometimes he appears to have created all nature for man alone; at others, he seems to have created man only as an object, whereon to exercise his arbitrary rage. Sometimes they are cherished by him, notwithstanding all their faults; at others, the whole species is condemned to eternal misery for an apple. This unchangeable God is alternately agitated by anger and love, revenge and pity, benevolence and fury. His conduct is continually destitute of that uniformity which characterises wisdom. Partial in his affections, he makes it the duty of his favourite people to commit deliberately the most atrocious crimes. He commands them to violate good faith, and contemn the rights of nations. He enjoins upon them the commission of robbery and murder. On other occasions, we see him forbidding the same crimes, ordaining justice and prescribing to mankind abstinence from whatever disturbs the good order of society. This God, who is in turn styled the God of *Vengeance*, the God of *Mercies*, the God of *Arms*, and the God of *Peace*, is ever at variance with himself. His subjects are consequently each one at liberty to copy

---

[8] The sacrifice of the Son of God is mentioned as a proof of his benevolence. Is it not rather a proof of his ferocity, cruelty, and implacable vengeance? A good Christian, on his death-bed said, "he had never been able to conceive how a good God could put ant innocent God to death, to appease a just God."

that part of his conduct which he finds most congenial to his humour. Hence their morality becomes arbitrary. It is surprising, that Christians have never yet been able to agree amongst themselves, whether it would be most pleasing to their God to tolerate the various opinions of mankind, or to exterminate all who differ from themselves. It is, in fact, a problem with them, whether it be most expedient to prosecute and assassinate those who think not as they do, or to treat them with humanity, and suffer them to live in peace.

Christians, however, do not fail to justify the strange and often iniquitous conduct attributed to their God in the Scriptures. This God, say they, being of right the absolute master of his creatures, can dispose of them at his pleasure. and for this no one can accuse him of injustice, or demand an account of his conduct. His justice is not the justice of mankind, and they have no right to censure any of his actions. It is easy to perceive the insufficiency of this answer. Mankind in making justice an attribute of their God, can have no idea of this virtue, but by supposing that it resembles the justice of their fellow-creatures. If God have a justice, which in its essence differs from that of man, we know not what it is, and we attribute to him a quality of which we have no idea. If it be said, that God owes nothing to his creatures, he is supposed to be a tyrant, whose conduct has no rule but his own caprice, and who cannot continue to be a model for us, seeing all relations must be reciprocal. If nothing be due from God to his creatures, how can any thing be due from them to him? If, as we are continually told. men are to God, *as the clay in the hands of the potter*, no moral relation can exist between them. It is, nevertheless, upon those relations that all religion is founded. Therefore, to say that God has no duty towards his creatures, and that his justice is different from that of mankind, is to sap the foundations of all religion and justice, which necessarily suppose that God ought to reward mankind for doing good, and punish them for doing evil.

In fine, how can the followers of the Christian system reconcile that barbarous conduct, and those sanguinary commands, attributed to him in the Scriptures, with his goodness or his wisdom? And how can goodness be an attribute of a God, who has created most of the human race only to damn them eternally?

Here we shall be told that the conduct of God is, to us, an impenetrable mystery, that we have no right to scrutinize it, and that our feeble reason must be lost whenever it attempts to sound the depth of divine wisdom. We are informed that we must adore in silence, and tremblingly submit to the oracles of a God, who has himself sufficiently made known his will in his holy Scriptures. This is what they call revelation, to which we proceed in the next chapter.

CHAP. V.

OF REVELATION.

HOW can we know, without the aid of reason, that God hath spoken? But, on the other side, is not reason proscribed by the Christian religion? Is not the use of reason forbidden, in the examination of the marvellous dogmas with which we are presented by this religion? Does it not continually exclaim against *a profane reason*, which it accuses of insufficiency, and often regards as rebellious to heaven? In order to be capable of judging of divine revelation, we must have a just idea of the Divinity. But seeing human reason is too weak and groveling to exalt itself to an acquaintance with the Supreme Being, from what source shall we derive that idea, beside revelation itself? Thus revelation itself is to become the proof of the authority of revelation.

Let us pass on from this conjurer's circle, and open the sacred books, destined to enlighten mankind, and before which reason must fall prostrate. Do they exhibit any precise ideas of the God, whose oracles they announce? Can we draw from them any just conceptions of its attributes? Is not this God represented as a mass of extraordinary qualities, which form an inexplicable enigma? If this revelation be, as is supposed, an emanation from God himself, who can confide in him? Does he not paint himself as false, unjust, deceitful, and cruel ; as setting snares for mankind; seducing, hardening, and leading them astray? [9] Thus the man, desirous of being assured of the truth of Christian revelation, finds himself, at the first step of enquiry, plunged into distrust and perplexity, which is increased by the indeterminable disputes of his sacred guides, who have never been able to agree upon the

---

[9] By the Scriptures and the Fathers of the Church, God is always represented as a seducer. He permits Eve to be seduced by a serpent. He hardens the heart of Pharaoh. Christ himself is a stone of stumbling. Such are the points of view under which the Divinity is exhibited to us.

manner of understanding the oracles of a Divinity which they say has revealed itself.

The hesitation and fear of the man who honestly examines the revelation adopted by Christians, must redouble, when he sees their God represented as revealing himself only to a few favourites of the human race, while he carefully conceals himself from the remainder, to whom, notwithstanding this, revelation is equally necessary. He must be uncertain whether or not he is of the number, to whom this partial God deigns to make himself known.

Most not his heart be troubled at the sight of a God, who vouchsafes to discover himself, and announce his decrees, only to a number or men, inconsiderable in comparison with the whole human race? Is he not tempted to accuse this God of a malevolence too dark, when he finds that for want of revealing himself to so many millions of mankind, he has caused their inevitable misery through an endless succession of ages? What ideas must he form to himself of a God who inflicts this punishment upon them for their ignorance of secret laws, which he has published by stealth in an obscure and unknown corner of Asia?

Thus Christians, even when they consult the Scriptures, find all things conspiring to put them on their guard against the God exhibited therein. Every thing inspires distrust of his moral character. All things float in an uncertainty. This God, in concert with the pretended interpreters of his will, seems to have the design of redoubling the darkness of his ignorance. He is, however, told, in order to appease his doubts, that the revealed will of God consists of mysteries; that is to say, things inaccessible to human understanding. In this case what need was there of having spoken? Ought a God to reveal himself to mankind for the sole purpose of not being comprehended? Is not such conduct as ridiculous as it is unreasonable? To say that God has revealed himself only to announce mysteries, is to say that he has revealed himself in order to remain unknown, to conceal from us his views, embarrass our understandings, and augment our ignorance and uncertainty.

A true revelation, proceeding from a just and good God, and necessary to all mankind, ought to be clear enough to be understood by all the human race. But will the revelation, upon which Judaism and Christianity are founded, bear the test of this criterion? The Elements of Euclid are intelligible to all who endeavour to understand them. This work excited no dispute among geometricians. Is it so with the Bible? and do its revealed truths occasion no disputes among divines? By what fatality have writings revealed by God himself still need of commentaries? and why do they demand additional lights from on high, before they can be believed or understood? Is it not astonishing, that what was intended as a guide for mankind, should be wholly above their comprehending? Is it not cruel, that what is of most importance to them should be least known? All is mystery, darkness, uncertainty, and matter of dispute, in a religion intended by the Most High, to enlighten the human race.

Far from contenting themselves with the pretended mysteries contained in the Scriptures, the priests of the Christian religion have, from age to age, invented new ones, which, though never mentioned by their God, their disciples are forced to believe. No Christian can entertain a doubt concerning the mysteries of the Trinity, the Incarnation, and the efficacy of sacraments; and yet Christ never explained these subjects. Among Christians every thing seems to be abandoned to the imagination, caprice, and arbitrary decision of priests, who arrogate to themselves the right of fabricating mysteries and articles of faith, as their interests occasionally require. Thus, this revelation perpetuates itself by means of the church, which pretends to be inspired by God, and which, far from enlightening the minds of her children, delights to confound, and plunges them in a sea of uncertainty.

Such are the effects of this revelation, which forms the basis of the Christian religion, and of the reality of which we are not permitted to doubt. God, it is said, has spoken to mankind. But when has he spoken? Thousands of years ago, by prophets and inspired men, whom he has chosen as organs of communication with mankind. But how can it be proved to have been God himself who spoke, except by having recourse to the testimony of the very persons who pretend to have received his commands? These interpreters of the divine will were then *men*; and are not men liable to be deceived themselves, and prone to deceive others? How then can we discover what confidence is due to the testimony which these organs of heaven give in favour of their own mission? How shall we be made sure that they have not been the dupes of some illusion, or an overheated imagination? At this remote period, how can we be certain that Moses conversed with God, and received from him the law which he communicated to the Hebrews? What was the temperament of this Moses? Was he phlegmatic or enthusiastic, honest or knavish, ambitious or disinterested, a practiser of truths or of falsehood? What confidence can be placed in the testimony of a man, who, after pretending to have performed so many miracles, could not convert his people from idolatry; and who, after having caused forty-seven thousand Israelites to perish by the sword, has the effrontery to assume the title of the *meekest of mankind*? Is it certain that the books which are attributed to Moses, and report so many miraculous circumstances, are perfectly authentic? In fine, what proof have we of its mission, except the testimony of a number of superstitious, ignorant, and credulous Israelites, who were probably the dupes of a ferocious legislator?

    What proofs does the Christian give us of the mission of Jesus Christ? Are we acquainted with his character and temperament? What degree of confidence can we place in the testimony of his disciples, who, by their own confession, were ignorant and unlearned men, and, consequently, liable to be imposed upon by the artifices of a dexterous impostor? Ought not the testimony of the most learned in Jerusalem to have greater weight with us, than that of the lowest vulgar, whose ignorance always renders them the dupes of those who endeavour to deceive them? These enquiries bring us to an examination of the proofs which are adduced in support of the Christian religion.

CHAP. VI.

THE PROOFS OF THE CHRISTIAN RELIGION, MIRACLES, PROPHECIES, AND MARTYRS.

WE have seen, in the preceding chapters, what just reasons there are to doubt the authenticity of the revelation of the Jews and Christians.

And further, relative to this article, Christianity has no advantage over any other religion.

All the religions on earth, notwithstanding their discordance, declare that they have emanated from God, and pretend to possess an exclusive right to his favours.

The Indian asserts, that the Brama himself is the author of his worship. The Scandinavian derives his from the awful Odin. If the Jew and the Christian have received theirs from Jehovah by the ministry of Moses and Jesus, the Mahometan affirms, that he has received his from his prophet, inspired by the same God. Thus all religions pretend to a divine origin; and they all interdict the use of reason in the examination of their sacred titles. Each pretends to be the only true one, to the exclusion of all others. All menace with the wrath of heaven those who refuse to submit to their authority, and all acquire the character of falsehood by the palpable contradictions with which they are filled ; by the misshapen, obscure, and often odious ideas which they give of the Godhead; by the whimsical laws, which they attribute to him, and by the disputes which they generate among their sectaries. In fine, they all appear to be a mass of impostors and reveries, equally disgusting to reason. Thus, on the score of pretensions, the Christian religion has no advantage over the other superstitions with which the world is infected, and its divine origin is contested by all others with as much propriety as theirs is denied by it.

How then shall we decide in its favour? How prove the validity of its pretensions? Has it any superior qualities, by which it merits the preference? And if so, what are they? Does it, better than any other, make us acquainted with the nature and essence of

God? Alas! it only renders them more incomprehensible. It represents him as a capricious tyrant, whose whimsies are sometimes favourable, but more commonly injurious to mankind. Does it render mankind better? Alas! it arms them against each other, renders them intolerant, and forces them to butcher their brethren. Does it render empires flourishing and powerful? Wherever it reigns, do we not see the people debased, destitute of energy, and ignorant of true morality? What then are the proofs which are to establish the superiority of the Christian religion over all others? We are answered, "miracles, prophecies, and martyrs." But these are to be found in all religions of the earth. There are in all nations men, who, being superior to the vulgar in science and cunning, deceive them with imposture, and dazzle them with performances which are judged to be supernatural, by men ignorant of the secrets of nature and the resources of art.

If the Jew cite the miracles of Moses, I see them performed before a people most ignorant, abject, and credulous, whose testimony has no weight with me. I may, also, suspect that these pretended miracles have been inserted in the sacred books of the Hebrews long after the death of those who might have testified the truth concerning them. If the Christians cite Jerusalem, and the testimony of Gallilee, to prove the miracles of Christ, I see them attested only by an ignorant populace; or I demand how it could be possible that an entire people, who had been witnesses to the miracles of Christ, should consent to his death, and even earnestly demand it? Would the people of London, or Paris, suffer a man who had raised the dead, restored the blind to sight, and healed the lame and paralytic, to be put to death before their eyes? If the Jews demanded the death of Jesus, all his miracles are at once annihilated in the mind of every unprejudiced person.

May not we, also, oppose to the miracles of Moses, and Christ, those performed by Mahomet in presence of all Mecca and Arabia assembled? The effect of his miracles was, at least, to convince the Arabians that he was a divine person. The miracles of Jesus convinced nobody of his mission. Saint Paul himself, who afterwards became the most ardent of his disciples, was not convinced by the miracles, of which, in his time, there existed so many witnesses. A new one was necessary for his conviction. And by what right do they at this day demand belief of miracles, which could not convince even in the time of the Apostles; that is to say, a short time after they were wrought?

Let it not be said that the miracles of Christ, are as well attested as any fact in profane history, and that to doubt them is as ridiculous as to doubt the existence of Scipio or Caesar, which we believe only on the report of the historians by whom they are mentioned. The existence or a man, of the general of an army, or an hero, is not improbable; neither is it a miracle.[10] We believe the probable facts, whilst we reject, with contempt, the miracles recounted by Titus Livius. The most stupid credulity is often joined to the most distinguished talents. Of this, the Christian religion furnishes us with innumerable examples. In matters of religion, all testimony is liable to suspicion. The most enlightened men see but ill, when they are intoxicated with enthusiasm, and dazzled by the chimeras of a wild imagination. A miracle is a thing impossible in the order of nature. If this be changed by God, he is not immutable.

It will probably be said, that, without changing the order of things, God and his favourites could find resources in nature unknown to mankind in general. But then their works would no longer be supernatural, and would have nothing of the marvellous. A miracle is an effect contrary to the established laws of nature. God himself, therefore, cannot perform miracles without counteracting the institutions of his own wisdom. A wise man, having seen a miracle, might with propriety doubt the evidence of his own senses. He ought carefully to examine, whether the extraordinary effect, which he does not comprehend, proceeds not

---

[10] A supernatural event requires, in order to be believed, much stronger proofs than a fact in no wise contradictory to probability. It is easy to believe, upon the testimony of Philostrates, that Appollonius existed, because his existence has nothing in it that shocks reason; but I will not believe Philostrates, when he tells me, that Appollonius performed miracles. I believe that Jesus Christ died; but I do not believe that he arose from the dead.

from some natural cause, whose manner of acting he does not understand.

But let us suppose, for a moment, that miracles may exist, and that those of Christ were real, or, at least, that they were inserted in the gospels by persons who imagined they had seen them. Are the witnesses who transmitted, or the Apostles who saw them, extremely deserving of credit? And have we not a right to refuse their testimonies? Were those witnesses very deserving men? By the confession of the Christians themselves they were ignorant men, taken from the dregs of the people, and consequently credulous and incapable of investigation. Were those witnesses disinterested? No; it was, undoubtedly, their chief interest to support those miracles, upon which were suspended the divinity of their master, and the truth of the religion they were endeavouring to establish. Are those miracles confirmed by the testimony of contemporary historians? Not one of them has mentioned those extraordinary facts. We find not a single Jew or Pagan in the superstitious city of Jerusalem, who heard even a word of the most marvelous facts that ever were recorded, and facts which happened in the midst of them. The miracles of Christ were ever attested by Christians only. We are requested to believe that, at the death of the Son of God, the earth quaked, the sun was darkened, and the dead arose. How does it happen that such extraordinary events have been noticed only by a handful of Christians? Were they the only persons who perceived them? We are told, also, that Christ arose from the dead; to prove which, they appeal to the testimony of his Apostles and followers. Would not one solemn apparition, in some public place, have been more decisive than all those clandestine ones, made to persons interested in the formation of a new sect? The Christian faith, according to St. Paul, is founded on the resurrection of Christ. This, then, ought to have been demonstrated to mankind, in the clearest and most indisputable manner.[11]

---

[11] The Basilidians and Cerinthians, heretics who lived in the infancy of Christianity, maintained that Jesus was not dead, and that Simon the Cyrenian was crucified in his place. See Epiph. *Haer.* c. 28. Thus, there were men, from

Have we not room to accuse the Saviour of the world with want of benevolence, in showing himself only to his disciples and favourites? It seems that he did not desire that all the world should believe in him. The Jews, it is said, deserve to be blinded for putting Christ to death. But, if this be the case, why did the apostles preach to them the gospel? Could it be expected that the Jews would believe the report of the apostles, rather than their own eyes?

Miracles appear to have been invented to supply the want of good reasons. Truth and evidence have no need of miracles to ensure their reception. Is it not very astonishing that God Almighty should find it easier to derange the order of nature, than to convince mankind of truths the most evident, and calculated to force their assent? Miracles were made to prove things which it is impossible to believe. There is no need of miracles when we talk of reason. Things incredible are here adduced in proof of incredible things. Almost all impostors who have fabricated religions, have announced incredibilities to mankind. They have afterwards fabricated miracles in proof of those incredibilities. "You cannot comprehend," said they, "what I tell you; but I will clearly prove to you that I tell the truth, by doing things that you cannot comprehend." People have in all ages been overcome by this brilliant reasoning. A passion for the marvelous has prevented enquiry. Mankind have not perceived that miracles could neither prove impossibilities, nor change the essence of truth. Whatever wonders a man, or, if you please, a God may perform, they can never prove that two and two are not four, or that three are no more than one. They cannot prove that an immaterial being, destitute of organs, has spoken to man; or that a good, wise, and just Being has commanded the execution of injustice, folly, and cruelty. It appears, therefore, that miracles prove nothing, unless it be the address and imposture of those who are desirous of profiting by the stupid credulity of mankind, and endeavour to

---

the of the church, who doubted the crucifixion, and. consequently the resurrection of Christ; and yet we are exhorted to believe them at the present day.

seduce them into a belief of the most extravagant falsehoods. Such men have always begun by falsely pretending to have an intimate commerce with God, in order to prove which, they have performed wonders that they attribute to the Being by whom they say they were commissioned. Every man, who performs miracles, endeavours to establish, not truth, but falsehood. Truth is simple and evident; the marvellous is ever to be suspected. Nature is always true to herself; she acts by unvarying laws. To say that God performs miracles, is to say that he contradicts himself, and violates the laws which he has prescribed to nature. It is to say, that he renders useless human reason, of which he is the author. Impostors alone can pronounce it necessary to discredit experience and reject reason.

Thus, the pretended miracles of the Christian, as well as all other religions, have no foundation, but the ignorance, credulity, and enthusiasm of mankind, and the cunning of impostors. The same may be said of prophecies. Mankind are ever anxious to pry into futurity; and there are always some kind individuals disposed to aid them in the gratification of this desire. There have been enchanters, divines, and prophets, in all the nations of the earth. The Jews have not been happier, in this respect, than others. Tartars, Negroes, and Indians have their share of impostors. All societies will find deceivers enough, so long as they are willing to pay for deception.

These inspired men have not been ignorant, that their prophecies ought to be extremely vague and ambiguous, in order that they might not, in process of time, appear to have been falsehoods. We need not, therefore, be surprised, that the Jewish prophecies are very dark, and of such a nature, that any thing may be found in them which interpreters think proper to seek. Those which are attributed to Christ, by his followers, are not considered in the same light by the Jews, who still expect the Messiah, whom the former believe to have been on earth eighteen centuries ago. The Jewish prophecies uniformly announce the deliverer of a discontented and oppressed nation. Such a one was also expected by the Romans, and almost all the nations of the earth. All mankind have a natural propensity to hope for a termination of the evils they suffer, and believe that Providence cannot, in justice, fail to render them, one day, happy. The Jews, the most superstitious nation on earth, building upon the supposed promise of their God, have always expected the coming of a monarch or conqueror, who is to elevate them from disgrace, and crown them with triumph. It was impossible for them to see this deliverer in the person of Jesus, who, instead of being the restorer of the Hebrew nation, was its destroyer; and since whose coming, they seem to have lost all favour with God.

It is asserted, that the destruction of the Jewish nation, and the dispersion of the Jews, were themselves foretold, and that they furnish a convincing proof of the truth of Christian prophecy. To this I answer, it was easy to foretell the dispersion and destruction of a restless, turbulent, and rebellious people, continually torn and convulsed by intestine divisions. Besides, this people was often conquered and dispersed. The temple destroyed by Titus, had previously suffered the same fate from Nebuchadnezzar, who carried the captive tribes into Assyria, and spread them through his territories. The dispersion of the Jews is more perceptible than that of other conquered nations, because they have generally, after a certain time, become confounded with their conquerors; whereas the Jews refuse to intermingle, by domestic connections, with the nations where they reside, and have religiously maintained this distinction. It is not the same with the *Cuebres* or *Parsis*, of Persia and Indostan, as well as the Armenians, who dwell in Mahometan countries! The Jews remain dispersed, because they are unsocial, intolerant, and blindly attached to their superstitions. [12]

Thus Christians have no reason to boast of the prophecies contained in the books of the Jews, nor to make invidious

---

[12] The Acts of the Apostles evidently prove, that, even before the time of Jesus, the Jews began to be dispersed. Jews came from Greece, Persia, Arabia. &c. to the feast of Pentecost. Acts, c. ii. 8. So that, after Jesus, the inhabitants of Judea only were dispersed by the Romans.

applications of them to that nation, because they detest its religion.

Judea was always subjected to priests, who had great influence over affairs of state. They were always meddling with politics, and undertook to foretell the events, fortunate or unfortunate, which were to befall the nation. No country was ever more fertile in prophets. This description of men instituted schools, where they initiated into the mysteries of their art those who proved themselves worthy of that honour, by discovering a wish to deceive a credulous people, and by such honest means acquire riches and respect. [13]

The art of prophesying was then an actual profession, or an useful and profitable branch of commerce in that miserable nation, which believed God to be incessantly busied in their affairs. The great gains resulting from this traffic of imposture must have caused divisions among the Jewish prophets. Accordingly, we find them crying down each other. Each one treated his rivals as false prophets, inspired by evil spirits. There have always been quarrels among impostors, to decide who should have the exclusive right of deceiving mankind.

If we examine the conduct of the boasted prophets of the Old Testament, we shall find them far from being virtuous persons. We see arrogant priests continually meddling with affairs of state, and interweaving them with religion. We see in them seditious subjects, incessantly caballing against all sovereigns, who were not sufficiently submissive to them. They cross their projects, excite their subjects to rebellion, effect their destruction, and thus accomplish the fatal predictions, which they had before made

---

[13] Saint Jerome says, that the Sadducees did not adopt the prophets, but contented themselves with believing the five books of Moses. Dodwell, *De Jure Laicorum*, asserts, that the prophets prepared themselves to prophesy by drinking wine. See page 259. It seems they were jugglers, poets, and musicians, who had made themselves masters of their trades, and knew how to exercise them profitably.

against them. [14]Such is the character of most of the prophets, who have played a part in the history of the Jews.

The studied obscurity of the prophecies is such, that those which are commonly applied to the Messiah, or the deliverer of Israel, are equally applicable to every enthusiast or prophet that appeared in Jerusalem or Judea. Christians, heated with the idea of Christ, think they meet him in all places, and pretend to see him in the darkest passages of the Old Testament. Deluding themselves by force of allegories, subtilties, commentaries, and forced interpretations, they have discovered the most formal predictions in all the vague oracles and nonsensical trash of the prophets. [15]

---

[14] The prophet Samuel displeased with Saul, who refused to second his cruelty, declared that he had forfeited the crown, and raised up a rival to him in the person of David. Elias appears to have been a seditious subject, who, finding himself unable to succeed in his rebellious designs, thought proper to escape due punishment by flight. Jeremiah himself gives us to understand that he conspired with the Assyrians against his besieged country. He seems to have employed himself in depriving his fellow-citizens of both the will and the courage to defend themselves. He purchased a field of his relations, at the very time when he informed his countrymen that they were about to be dispersed, and led away in captivity. The king of Assyria recommends this prophet to his general, Nebuzaradan, whom he commands to take great care of him.--See Jeremiah.

[15] Any thing may be found in the Bible, if it be read with the imagination of Saint Augustine, who pretended to see all the New Testament in the Old. According to him, the death of Abel is a type of that of Christ; the two wives of Abraham are the synagogue and the church; a piece of red cloth held up by an harlot, who betrayed Jericho, signifies the blood of Christ; the lamb, goat, and lion, are figures of Jesus Christ; the brazen serpent represents the sacrifice on the cross. Even the mysteries of the Christian religion are announced in the Old Testament. Manna represents the Eucharist, &c. See S. Aug. *Serm.* 78, and *Ep.* 156. How can a man, in his senses, see, in the Immanuel announced by Isaiah, the Messiah, whose name is Jesus? Isaiah c. vii. v. 14. How discover, in an obscure and crucified Jew, a leader who shall govern Israel? How see a royal deliverer and restorer of the Jews, in one, who, far from delivering his nation, came only to destroy their laws; and after whose coming their land was desolated by the Romans? A man must be sharp sighted indeed to find the Messiah in their predictions. Jesus himself does not seem to have been more

Men are not scrupulous respecting things which accord with their desires. When we examine, without prejudice, the prophecies of the Hebrews, we find them to be a misshapen mass of rhapsodies, the offspring of fanaticism and delirium. We find them obscure and enigmatical, like the oracles of the Pagans. In fine. it is evident that these pretended divine oracles are the vagaries and impostures of men, who imposed on the credulity of a superstitious nation which believes in dreams, visions, apparitions, and sorceries, and received with avidity any deception, provided it were sufficiently decorated with the marvelous. Wherever mankind are ignorant, there will be found prophets and workers of miracles, and these two branches of commerce will always decay in the same proportion as mankind become enlightened.

Among the proofs of the authenticity of their religion, Christians enumerate a multitude of *martyrs*, who have sealed with their blood their belief of the opinions they had embraced. There is no religion destitute of ardent defenders, who would sacrifice their lives for the opinions to which they believe their eternal happiness attached. Superstitious and ignorant men are obstinate in their prejudices. Their credulity prevents them from suspecting any deception in their spiritual guides. Their vanity persuades them that they are incapable of wavering; and if, in fine, their imaginations be strong enough to see the heavens open, and a recompense prepared therein for their courage, there is no torment they will not brave and endure. In their intoxication they will despise all torments of short duration; they will smile upon their executioners; and their souls, alienated from earthly things, will become insensible to pain. In such scenes, the hearts of

---

clear, or happy, in his prophecies. In the Gospel of Luke, chap. xxi. he speaks of the last judgment: he mentions angels, who, at the sound of the trumpet, assemble Mankind together before him. He adds: "Verily, I say unto you, this generation shall not pass away, until these things are accomplished." The world, however, still stands, and Christians have been expecting the last judgment for eighteen hundred years.

spectators are softened; they admire the astonishing firmness of the martyr; they catch his enthusiasm, and believe his cause just. His courage appearing to them supernatural and divine, becomes an indubitable proof of the truth of his opinions. Thus, by a sort of contagion, enthusiasm communicates itself. Men are always interested in the fate of those who show the greatest firmness; and tyranny always multiplies the friends of those whom it persecutes. The constancy of the first Christians must, therefore, have produced proselytes, by a natural effect of their conduct. Martyrs prove nothing, unless it be the strength of the enthusiasm, error, and obstinacy produced by superstition, and the barbarous folly of those who persecute their fellow-creatures for religious opinions.

Every violent passion has its martyrs. Pride, vanity, prejudice, love, patriotism, and even vice itself, produces martyrs; or, at least, a contempt of every kind of danger. Is it, then, surprising, that enthusiasm and fanaticism, the strongest passions of mankind, have so often enabled men, inspired with the hopes they give, to face and despise death?--Besides, if Christians can boast a catalogue of martyrs, Jews can do the same. The unfortunate Jews, condemned to the flames by the Inquisition, were martyrs to their religion; and their fortitude proves as much in its favour, as that of the Christians can do in favour of Christianity. If martyrs demonstrate the truth of a religion, there is no religion or sect which may not be looked upon as true.

In fine, among the perhaps exaggerated number of martyrs, boasted by Christians, many were rather the victims of an inconsiderate zeal, a turbulent and seditious spirit, than a real love of religion. The church itself does not presume to justify some, who, transported by a volcanic zeal, have troubled the peace of the earth, and poured out flaming destruction on all who differed in opinion from themselves; until mankind, consulting their own tranquillity and safety, have destroyed them. If men of this description were to be considered as martyrs, every disturber of society, when punished, would acquire a right to this title.

CHAP. VII.

OF THE MYSTERIES OF THE CHRISTIAN RELIGION.

TO reveal any thing to a man, is to discover to him secrets of which he was before ignorant. If we ask Christians what the secrets were, the importance of which rendered it necessary that they should be revealed by God himself, we shall be told that the greatest of those secrets, and the one most necessary to mankind, is the Unity of the Godhead; a secret which, say they, human wisdom could never have discovered of itself. But are we not at liberty to doubt the truth of this assertion? Moses, undoubtedly, declared an *only* God to the Hebrews, and did all in his power to render them enemies to the idolatry and polytheism of other surrounding nations, whose belief and whose modes of worship he represented as abominable in the eyes of the celestial Monarch, who had brought them out of the land of Egypt. But have not many wise men among the heathens discovered, without the assistance of the Jewish revelation, one supreme God, superior to all others? Moreover, was not Fate, to which all the other gods of the heathens were subordinate, an only God, to whose sovereign law all nature was subject? As to the colours in which Moses paints his Godhead, neither Jews nor Christians have a right to pride themselves therein. He is represented as a capricious and irascible despot, full of cruelty, injustice, partiality, and malignity. What kind of being shall we contemplate, when we add to this the ineffable attributes ascribed to him in the Christian Theology? Is the Godhead described when it is said that it is a *spirit*, an *immaterial* being, which resembles nothing presented to us by our senses? Is not human understanding confounded with the negative attributes of *infinity*, *immensity*, *eternity*, *omnipotence*, and *omniscience*, with which he has been decorated, only to render him still more incomprehensible? How can the wisdom, the goodness, justice, and other moral qualities of this God, be reconciled with that strange and often atrocious conduct, which are attributed to him in almost every page of the Old and New

Testament? Would it not have been better to have left mankind in entire ignorance of the Godhead, than to reveal to him a God made up of contradictions, which lead to eternal dispute, and serve only to trouble his repose? To reveal such a God to mankind, is only to discover to them the means to embarrass and render themselves wretched, and quarrel with and injure one another.

But, be this at it may, is it true that Christianity admits but one God, the same which was revealed by Moses? Do we not see Christians adore a threefold divinity, under the name of the *Trinity*? The supreme God begat from all eternity a son equal to himself; from these two proceeds a third equal to the two first; these three Gods, equal in perfection, divinity, and power, form, nevertheless, only one God. To overturn this system, it seems sufficient only to show its absurdity. Is it but to reveal such mysteries as these that the Godhead has taken pains to instruct mankind? Have opinions more absurd and contrary to reason ever existed among the most ignorant and savage nations?[16] In the mean time, however, the writings of Moses contain nothing that could authorise the construction of a system so wild. It is only by having recourse to the most forced explanations, that the doctrine of the Trinity is pretended to be found in the Bible. As to the

---

[16] The dogma of the Trinity is evidently borrowed from the reveries of Plato, or from the allegories under which that romantic Philosopher chose to conceal his doctrine. It appears that to him the Christian religion is indebted for the greater part of its dogmas. Plato admitted three Hypostases, or modes of being in the Divinity. The first constituted the supreme God; the second the Logos, Word, or divine intelligence proceeding from the first; the third is the Spirit, or Soul of the World. The early teachers of the Christian religion appear to have been Platonics; their enthusiasm probably found in Plato a doctrine analogous to their feelings; had they been grateful, they would have recorded him as a prophet, or at least as one of the fathers of the church. The Jesuitical missionaries found a Divinity, nearly similar to that of the Christians, at Thibet. Among the Tartars, God is called Kon-cio-cik, the only God, and Kon-cio-sum, the threefold God. They also give him the titles Om, Ha, Hum, intelligence, might, power or words, heart, love. The number three was always revered among the ancients; because Salom, which in the oriental languages signifies three, signifies also health, safety, salvation.

Jews, contented with the *only God* which their legislator has declared to them, they have never attempted to create a *threefold one*.

The second of these Gods, or, according to the Christians, *the second person of the Trinity*, having clad himself with human nature, and become incarnate in the womb of a virgin, he submitted himself to the infirmities of our species, and even suffered an ignominious death to expiate the sins of the earth. This is what Christians call the *mystery of Incarnation*. He must be indeed blind, who cannot see these absurd notions are borrowed from the Egyptians, Indians, and Grecians, whose ridiculous mythologies describe gods as possessing human forms, and subject to infirmities, like mankind. [17]

Thus, we are commanded by Christianity to believe that a God having become man without doing injury to his divine nature, has suffered, died, and offered himself a sacrifice to himself; and all this was absolutely and indispensibly necessary to appease his own wrath. This is what Christians denominate the *mystery of the redemption* of the human race.

This dead God, however, was resuscitated. Thus the Adonis of the Phenicians, the Osiris of the Egyptians, and the Atys of the Phrygians, are represented as periodically resigning and re-assuming life. The God of the Christians rises again, reanimated, and bursts the tomb, triumphant.

Such are the wondrous secrets, or sublime mysteries, that the Christian religion unfolds to its disciples. So great, so abject, and so ever incomprehensible are the ideas it gives us of the divine Being. Such is the illumination our minds receive from revelation! A revelation which only serves to render still more impenetrable the clouds which veil the divine essence from human eyes. God,

---

[17] The Egyptians appear to have been the first, who pretended that their gods had assumed material bodies. Foe, the god of the Chinese, was born of a virgin, who was fecundated by a ray of the sun. In Indostan nobody doubts the incarnations of Vishnou. It seems that theologists of all nations, despairing to exalt themselves to a level with God, have endeavoured to debase him to level with themselves.

we are told, is willing to render himself inconsistent and ridiculous, to confound the curiosity of those whom, we are at the same time informed, he desires to enlighten by his special grace. What must we think of a revelation which, far from teaching us any things, is calculated to darken and puzzle the clearest ideas?

Thus, notwithstanding the boasted revelation of the Christians, they know nothing of that Being whom they make the basis of their religion. On the contrary, it only serves to obscure all the notions which might otherwise be formed of him. In holy writ he is called an hidden God. David tells us, that he places his dwelling in darkness, that clouds and troubled waters form the pavilion with which he is covered. In fine, Christians, although enlightened, as they say, by God himself, have only ridiculous and inconsistent ideas of him, which render his existence doubtful, or even impossible, in the eyes of every man who consults his reason.

What notions, indeed, can we form of a God, who, after having created the world solely for the happiness of mankind, nevertheless buffers the greater part of the human race to be miserable both in this world and that which is to come? How can a God, who enjoys a Supreme felicity, be offended with the actions of his creatures? This God is then susceptible of grief; his happiness can be disturbed; he is then dependant on man, who can, at pleasure, delight or afflict him! How can a benevolent God bestow on his creatures a fatal liberty by the abuse of which they may incur his anger, and their own destruction? How can that Being, who is himself the author of life and nature, suffer death? How can an only God become triple without injuring his unity? We shall be answered, that all these matters are mysteries; but such mysteries destroy even the existence of God. It would be more reasonable to admit, with Zoroaster, or Manes, two principles or opposite powers in nature, than to believe, with Christians, that there is an *omnipotent* God, who *cannot* prevent the existence of evil; a God who is *just*, and yet partial; a God all merciful, and yet so implacable, that he will punish through an eternity the crimes of a moment; an *only* God, who is *threefold*; a God, the chief of beings, who consents to die, being unable to satisfy by any other means his divine justice. If, in the same subject, contraries cannot subsist at the same time, either the existence of the God of the Jews, or that of the Christians, must undoubtedly be impossible. Whence we are forced to conclude, that the teachers of Christianity, by means of the attributes with which they have decorated or rather disfigured their Godhead, have, in fact, annihilated the God of the Jews, or at least so transformed him, that he is no longer the same. Thus, revelation, with all its fables and mysteries, has only embarrassed the reason of mankind, and rendered uncertain the simple notions which they might form to themselves of that *necessary Being*, who governs the universe with immutable laws. Though the existence of a God cannot be denied, it is yet certain that reason cannot admit the existence of the one which the Christians adore, and whose conduct, commands, and qualities, their religion pretends to reveal. If they are Atheists, who have no ideas of the *Supreme Being*, the Christian theology must be looked upon as a project invented to destroy his existence. [18]

---

[18] Divines have always disagreed among themselves respecting the proofs of the existence of a God. They mutually style each other Atheists, because their demonstrations have never been the same. Few Christians have written on the existence of God, without drawing upon themselves an accusation of Atheism. Descartes, Clarke, Pascal, Arnauld, and Nicole, have been considered as Atheists. The reason is plain. It is impossible to prove the existence of a Being so inconsistent as the God of the Christians. We shall be told that men have no means for judging of the Divinity, and that our understandings are too narrow to form any idea of him. Why then do they dispute incessantly concerning him? Why assign to him qualities which destroy each other? Why recount fables concerning him? Why quarrel and cut each others throats, because they are differently interpreted by different persons?

CHAP. VIII.

MYSTERIES AND DOGMAS OF CHRISTIANITY.

NOT content with having enveloped their God in mysterious clouds and Judaic fables, the teachers of Christianity seem to be still busied in the multiplication of mysteries, and embarrassing more and more the reason of their disciples. Religion, designed to enlighten mankind, is only a tissue of enigmas; a labyrinth which sound sense can never explore. That which ancient superstitions found most incomprehensible, seems not unaptly to be interwoven with a religious system, which imposes eternal silence on reason. The fatalism of the Grecians has been transformed, in the hands of Christian priests, into predestination. According to this tyrannic dogma, the God of mercies has destined the greatest part of mankind to eternal torments. He places them in this world that they, by the abuse of their faculties and liberty, may render themselves worthy of the implacable wrath of their creator. A benevolent and prescient God gives to mankind *a free will*, of which he knows they will make so perverse an use, as to merit eternal damnation. Thus, instead of punishing them with the propensities necessary to their happiness, he permits them to act, only that he may have the pleasure of plunging them into hell. Nothing, can be more horrid than the description given us by Christians of this place, destined to be the future residence of almost all mankind. There a merciful God will, throughout an eternity, bathe himself in the tears of wretches, whom he created for misery. Sinners, shut up in this awful dungeon, will be delivered up for ever to devouring flames. There shall be heard weeping, and wailing, and gnashing of teeth. The torments of this place shall, at the end of millions of years, have only begun. The consoling hope of a distant mitigation of pain shall be unknown. In one word, God, by an act of his omnipotence, shall render man capable of miseries uninterrupted, and interminable. His justice will punish finite crimes, the effects of which are limited by time, by torments infinite in degree and duration. Such is the idea a Christian forms of the God that demands his love. This tyrant creates him only to render him miserable; he gives him reason to deceive him, and propensities to lead him astray. He gives him liberty, that he may incur eternal ruin. He gives him advantages above the beasts, that he may be subjected to torments, which beasts, like inanimate substances, are incapable of suffering. The dogma of predestination represents the lot of man as worse than, that of brutes and stones. [19]

It is true, the Christian religion promises a blissful residence to those whom God shall have chosen to be objects of his love. But this place is reserved only for a small number of *elect*, who, without any merit in themselves, shall, nevertheless, have unbounded claims upon the grace of God.

Thus, the Tartarus and Elysium of the heathen mythology, invented by impostors to awe and seduce mankind, have been transplanted into the system of the Christians, who have given them the new appellation of Heaven and Hell.

The followers of the Christian religion believe in a race of invisible beings, different from man and subordinate to God, part of whom is employed in executing the wrath of God upon offenders; and part in watching over his works, and particularly the preservation of man. The former, being malevolent spirits, are called *devils*, *demons*, &c., the latter, being benevolent spirits, are called angels. They are supposed to leave the faculty of rendering

---

[19] The doctrine of predestination was also a tenet of the Jews. In the writings of Moses, a God is exhibited, who, in his decrees, is partially fond of a chosen people, and unjust to all others. The theology and history of the Greeks represent men as punished for necessary crimes, foretold by oracles. Of this Orestes, Oedipus, Ajax, &c. are examples. Mankind have always described God as the most unjust of all beings. According to the Jansenists, God bestows his grace on whom he pleases, without any regard to merit. This is much more conformable to the Christian, Pagan, and Jewish fatalism, than the doctrine of the Molinists, that God grants his grace to all who ask and deserve it. It is certain that Christians in general are true fatalists. They evade this accusation, by declaring that the designs of God are mysteries. If so, why do they eternally dispute about them?

themselves sensible, and taking the human form. Good angels are, in the imagination of Christians, what the Nymphs, Lares, and Pernates, were imagined to be by the heathens, and what the Fairies were with writers of romances. The sacred books of the Jews and Christians are replete with these marvellous beings, whom God has sent to his favourites to be their guides, protectors, and tutelar deities.

Devils are considered as the enemies and seducers of the human race, and perpetually busied in drawing them into sin. A power is attributed to them of performing miracles, similar to those wrought by the Most High; and, above, a power that counteracts his, and renders all his projects abortive. In fact, the Christian religion does not formally allow the same power to the devil as to God; nevertheless, it supposes that malevolent Being prevents mankind from entering into the enjoyment of the felicity destined them by the goodness of God, and leads most of them into eternal Perdition. Christians, however, do virtually attribute to the devil an empire much more extensive than that of the Supreme Being. The latter, with difficulty, saves a few elect; while the former carries off, in spite of him, the greater part of mankind, who listen to his destructive temptations, rather than the absolute commands of God. This Satan, the cause of so much terror to Christians, was evidently borrowed from the doctrine of two principles, formerly admitted in Egypt and all the East. The Osyris and Typhon of the Egyptians, the Orosmades and Aharimanes of the Persians and Chaldeans, have undoubtedly given birth to the continual war between the God of Christians and his formidable adversary. By this system mankind have endeavoured to account for all the good and evil with which life is chequered. An Almighty Devil serves to justify the Supreme Being with respect to all necessary and unremitted evils which afflict the human race.

Such are the dreadful and mysterious doctrines upon which Christians in general are agreed. There are many others which arc peculiar to different sects. Thus, a numerous sect of Christians admit an intermediate state between heaven and hell, where souls, too sinful for the former and too innocent for the latter, are subjected for a time, in order to expiate by their sufferings the sin they commit in this life; after undergoing this punishment, they are received into the abodes of eternal felicity. This doctrine, which was evidently drawn from the reveries of Plato, has, in the hands of the Roman priests, been converted into an inexhaustible source of riches. They have arrogated to themselves the power of opening the gates of purgatory, and pretend that, by their prayers, they can mitigate the rigour of the divine decrees, and abridge the torments of the souls, condemned to this place by a just God. [20]

The preceding remarks show, that the Christian religion has been often inculcated and spread by dint of terror. By striking mankind with horror they render them submissive, and remove all his dependence on his reason. [21]

---

[20] It is evident that the Roman Catholics are indebted to Plato for their Purgatory. That great philosopher divided souls into three classes; the pure, the curable, and the incurable. The first returned, by refusion, to the universal soul of the world, or the divinity, from which they had emanated; the second went to hell, where they passed in review every year before the judges of that dark empire, who suffered them to return to light when they had sufficiently expiated their faults; the incurables remained in Tartarus, where they were to suffer eternal torment. Plato, as well as Christian casuists, described the crimes, faults, &c. which merit those different degrees of punishment.

Protestant Divines, jealous probably of the riches of the Catholic clergy, have imprudently rejected the doctrine of a Purgatory, whereby they have much diminished their own credit. It would, perhaps, have been wiser to have rejected the doctrine of an hell, whence souls can never be released, than that of Purgatory, which is more reasonable, and from which the clergy can deliver souls by means of that all-powerful agent, money.

[21] Mahomet perceived, as well as Christian Divines, the necessity of frightening mankind, in order to govern them. "Those," says the Alcoran, "who do not believe, shall be clothed in a garment of fire; boiling water shall be poured on their heads; their skins and their entrails shall be smitten with rods of iron. Whenever they shall Strive to escape from hell, and avoid its torments, they shall be thrust again into it; and the devils say unto them: 'taste the pain of burning'." See Alcoran, ch. viii.

CHAP. IX.

OF THE RITES AND MYSTERIOUS CEREMONIES OR THEURGY OF THE CHRISTIANS.

IF the doctrines of the Christian religion be mysteries inaccessible to reason; if the God it announces be inconceivable, we ought not to be surprised at seeing the rites and ceremonies of this religion mysterious and unintelligible. Concerning a God, who hath revealed himself only to confound human reason, all things must necessarily be incomprehensible and unreasonable.

The most important ceremony of the Christian religion is called baptism. Without this, no man, it is held, can be saved. It consists in pouring water on the infant or adult, with an invocation on the name of the Trinity. By the mysterious virtue of this water, and the words by which it is accompanied, the person is spiritually regenerated. He is cleansed from the stains, transmitted through successive generations, from the father of the human race. In a word, he becomes a child of God, and is prepared to enter into his glory at death. Now, it is said, that the death of man is the effect of the sin of Adam; and if, by baptism, sin be effaced, why is man still subject to death? But here we are told, it is from the spiritual, not bodily death, that Christ has delivered mankind. Yet this spiritual death is only the death of sinfulness. In this ease, how does it happen that Christians continue to sin, as if they had never been redeemed and delivered from sin? Whence it results, that baptism is a mystery impenetrable to reason; and its efficacy is disproved by experience. [22]

In some Christian sects, a bishop or pontiff, by pronouncing a few words, and applying a few drops of oil to the forehead,

---

[22] The ceremony of baptism was practised in the mysteries of Mythias, and those initiated were thereby regenerated. This Mythias was also a mediator. Although Christian divines consider baptism necessary to salvation, we find Paul would not suffer the Corinthians to he baptised. We also learn that he circumcised Timotheus.

causes the spirit to descend upon whom he pleases. By this ceremony the Christian is *confirmed* in the faith, and receives invisibly a profusion of graces from the Most High. Those who wandering farthest from reason, have entered most deeply into the spirit of the Christian religion, not contented with the dark mysteries common to other sects, have invented one still darker amid more astonishing, which they denominate transubstantiation. At the all-powerful command of a priest, the God of the Universe is forced to descend from the habitation of his glory, and transform himself into a piece of bread. This bread is afterwards worshipped by a people, who boast their detestation of idolatry. [23]

In the puerile ceremonies, so highly valued by Christians, we cannot avoid seeing the plainest traces of the *Theurgy* practised among the Orientals, where the Divine Being, compelled by the magic power of certain words and ceremonies uttered by priests, or other persons initiated into the necessary secret, descends to earth and performs miracles. This sort of magic is also exercised among Christian priests. They persuade their disciples that, by certain arbitrary actions, and certain movements of the body, they can oblige the God of Nature to suspend his laws, give himself up to their desires, and load them with every favour they choose to demand. Thus, in this religion, the priest assumes the right of commanding God himself. On this empire over their God, this real Theurgy, or mysterious commerce with heaven, are founded those puerile and ridiculous ceremonies which Christians call *sacraments*. We have already seen this Theurgy in Baptism, Confirmation, and the Eucharist. We find it, also, in *penitence*, or the power which the priests of some sects arrogate to themselves,

---

[23] The Bramas of Indostan, distribute a kind of grain in their Pagodas; this distribution is called Prajadim, or Eucharist. The Mexicans believe in a kind of transubstantiation, which is mentioned by father Acosta. See his Travels, chap. 24. The Protestants have had the courage to reject transubstantiation, although it is formally established by Christ, who says, "Take, eat; this is my body." Averoes said: "Anima mea fit cum philosophis, non vero cum Christianis, gente stolidissima, qui Deum faciunt et comedunt. The Peruvians have a religious ceremony, in which, after sacrificing a lamb, they mingle his blood with flour, and distribute it amongst the people.--Alnetanae quest. lib. ii. cap. 20.

of remitting, in the name of Heaven, all sins confessed to them. It as seen in *orders*, that is to say, in the ceremony which impresses on certain men a sacred character, by which they are ever after distinguished from profane mortals. It is seen in the rites and functions which torture the last moments of the dying. It is seen in marriage, which natural union, it is supposed, cannot meet with the approbation of Heaven, unless the ceremony of a priest render it valid, and procure it the sanction of the Most High. [24]

We see this Theurgy, or *white magic*, in the prayers, forms, liturgies, and, in short, in all the ceremonies of the Christians. We find it in their opinion, that words disposed in a certain manner can influence the will All of God, and oblige him to change his immutable decrees. Its efficacy is seen in *exorcisms*, that is, ceremonies, in which, by means of a magic water and some mysterious words, it is pretended that evil spirits which infest mankind can be expelled. *Holy water*, which has taken the place of the *aqua lustralis* of the Romans, is believed by certain Christians to possess astonishing virtues. It renders sacred, places and things which were profane. In fine, the Christian Theurgy being employed by a pontiff in the consecration of a king, renders him more respectable in the eyes of men, and stamps him with a divine character.

Thus all is magic and mystery, all is incomprehensible, in a religion revealed by God himself, to enlighten the darkened understanding of mankind.

---

[24] The number of Roman Catholic sacraments, seven; a cabalistic, magic, and mysterious number.

CHAP. X.

OF THE INSPIRED WRITINGS OF THE CHRISTIANS.

CHRISTIANS endeavour to prove the divine origin of their religion by certain writings, which they believe to be sacred, and to have been inspired by God himself. Let us them see if these writings do really exhibit marks of that wisdom, omniscience, and perfection which we attribute to the Divinity.

The Bible, every word of which, Christians believe to have been dictated by inspiration, is composed of an incongruous collection of the sacred writings of the Hebrews, called the Old Testament; to which are added, a number of works, more recent indeed, but of equal inspiration, known by the name of the New Testament. At the head of this collection are five books which are attributed to Moses, who was, it is said, in writing them, the secretary of God. He therein goes back to the origin of things. He attempts to initiate us into the mystery of the creation of the world, of which he has only the most vague and confused ideas. He betrays at every word a profound ignorance of the laws of Nature. God, according to Moses, created the sun, which, in our planetary system, is the source of light, several days after he had created the light. God, who can be represented by no image, created man in his own image. He creates him *male* and *female*; but, soon forgetting what he had done, he creates woman from one of the ribs of the man. In one word, we see, at the very entrance of the Bible, nothing but ignorance and contradiction. [25]It appears, at once, that the cosmogony of the Hebrews is only a tissue of fables and allegories, incapable of giving any true idea of things, and calculated to please only a savage and ignorant people,

---

[25] St. Augustin confesses that there is no way of preserving the true sense of the three first chapters of Genesis without wronging religion and attributing things to God which are unworthy of him; and declares, that recourse must be had to Allegory. *Aug. de Genesi, contra Machineos.* Origen, also, grants, if we take the history of the Bible literally, it is absurd and contradictory. *Philos.* p. 12.

destitute of science, and unqualified for reasoning. In the rest of the writings of Moses, we see little but a string of marvellous and improbable stories, and a mass of ridiculous and arbitrary laws. The author concludes with giving an account of his own death. The books posterior to Moses exhibit equal ignorance. Joshua stops the sun, which did not move. Sampson, the Jewish Hercules, has strength to overthrow a temple.--But we should never finish the enumeration of the fables and falsehoods of these books, which are audaciously attributed to the Holy Ghost. The story of the Hebrews presents us only with a mass of tales, unworthy the gravity of history and the majesty of Divinity. Ridiculous to reason, it appears to have been invented only to amuse the credulity of a stupid and infant people.

This strange compilation is intermingled with obscure and unconnected oracles, with which different prophets have, from time to time, enriched Jewish superstition. Every thing in the Old Testament breathes enthusiasm, fanaticism, and delirium, often decorated with pompous language. There, every thing is to be found, except good sense, good logic, and reason, which seems to be absolutely excluded from the books which guide the conduct of the Hebrews and Christians.

We have already mentioned the abject, and often absurd ideas of God, which are exhibited in the Bible. In this book, all his conduct appears ridiculous. He blows hot and cold, and contradicts himself every moment. He acts imprudently, and then repents of what he had done. He supports with one hand, and destroys with the other. After having punished all the human race with death, for the sins of man, he declares, by Ezekiel, that he is just, and will not render children responsible for the iniquities of their fathers. He commands the Hebrews, by the mouth of Moses, to rob the Egyptians. In the decalogue, published by Moses, theft and murder are forbidden. In short, Jehovah, ever in contradiction with himself, varies with circumstances, preserves no uniformity of conduct, and is represented in the books, said to be inspired by his spirit, as a tyrant, which the most decided villain would blush to be.

When we cast our eyes over the New Testament, there, also, we see nothing characteristic of that spirit of truth which to said to have dictated this work. Four historians, or fabulists. have written the marvellous history of the Messiah. Seldom agreeing with respect to the circumstances of his life, they sometimes contradict each other in the most palpable manner. The genealogy of Christ, given us by Matthew, differs widely from that given us by Luke. One of the Evangelists says, that Christ was carried into Egypt; whilst, by another, this event is not even hinted at. One makes the duration of his mission three years, while another represents it as only as many months. We do not find them at all better accord, respecting the facts in general which they report. Mark says that Christ died at the third hour, that is to say, nine o'clock in the morning; John says, that he died at the sixth hour, that is, at noon. According to Matthew and Mark, the women who, after the death of Jesus, went to his sepulchre, saw only one angel; whereas, according to Luke and John, they saw two. These angels were, by some, said to be within the tomb; by others, without. Several of the miracles of Jesus are also differently reported by the Evangelists. This is likewise the case with his appearances after his resurrection. Ought not all these things to excite a doubt of the infallibility of the Evangelists, and the reality of their divine inspirations? What shall we say of the false and forged prophecies, applied to Christ in the gospel? Matthew pretends that Jeremy foretold that Christ should be betrayed for thirty pieces of silver; yet no such prophecy is to be found in Jeremiah. Nothing is more singular than the manner in which Christian divines evade these difficulties. Their solutions are calculated to satisfy only those who conceive it their duty to remain in blindness.[26] Every man of sense must feel, that all the industry and sophism on earth can never reconcile such palpable contradictions; and the efforts of interpreters serve only to show

---

[26] Jerome himself says, that the quotations of Matthew do not agree with the Greek version of the Bible. Erasmus is obliged to confess, that the Holy Spirit permitted the Apostles to go astray.

the weakness of their cause. Is it, then, by subterfuges, subtleties, and falsehoods, that we are to render service to God?

We find equal errors and contradictions in the pompous gasconade and declamatory bombast of St. Paul. The epistles and harangues of this man, inspired by the Spirit of God, appear to be the enthusiastic ravings of a madman. The most laboured commentaries have, in vain, endeavoured to reconcile the contradictions with which his work are filled, and the inconsistency of his conduct, which sometimes favoured and sometimes opposed Judaism.[27] We do not find ourselves more enlightened by the works attributed to the other Apostles. It seems as if these persons, inspired by the Holy Ghost, came on the earth only to prevent their disciples from comprehending what they had been sent to teach them.

At the foot of the collection, which forms the New Testament, we find the mystic work known by the name of the Revelation of St. John. This is an unintelligible thing, in which the author has endeavoured to collect and concentrate all the gloomy and dreadful ideas contained in the rest of the Bible. It exhibits to the wretched race of Man the awful and approaching

---

[27] St. Paul himself informs us, that he was ravished up to the third heaven. Why was he transported thither, and what did he learn by his journey? Things unspeakable which no man could comprehend. What advantage are mankind to derive from all this? St. Paul, in the Acts of the Apostles, is guilty of a falsehood, in saying before the high priest, that he is persecuted, because he is a Pharisee, and on account of the resurrection. Here are two untruths. First, because Paul was, at that time, the most zealous apostle of the Christian religion, and consequently a Christian. Secondly, because the accusations brought against him did not refer to his opinion on resurrection. If we know that the Apostles sometimes wandered from the truth, how shall we believe them at others? Further, we see this great Apostle continually changing his counsels and conduct. At Jerusalem, he point blank opposes Peter, who favoured Judaism; whereas he himself afterwards complied with Jewish rites. In fine, he always accommodates himself to the circumstances of the time, and becomes all things to all men. He seems to have set an example to the Jesuits, of their conduct in the Indies, with which they are reproached, where they unite the worship of the Pagans to that of Christ.

end of a perishing world. It is filled with horrid pictures, by gazing on which, the trembling Christian becomes petrified with fear and wonder, indifferent to life, and useless, or an incumbrance to society. Thus, in a manner not unworthy of itself, terminates this compilation, so inestimable and adorable to Christians, so ridiculous and contemptible to the man of reason, so unworthy of a good and bounteous God; so detestable to him who contemplates the unparalleled evils it has occasioned on the earth.

Having taken for the rule of their conduct and opinions a Book so full of blasphemous fables and striking contradictions concerning God, Christians have never agreed in the interpretation of his will, or precisely known what he exacted from them. Thus they have made this obscure work a bone of contention, an inexhaustible source of quarrels, a common arsenal, where all contending parties have supplied themselves with arms for mutual destruction. Geometricians dispute not concerning the fundamental principles of their science. By what fatality does it happen that Christian revelation, the foundation of a religion on which depends the eternal felicity of man, should be unintelligible, subject to disputes, and often deluge the earth with blood? To judge by effects, such a revelation ought rather to he thought the work of a malign spirit, a genius of darkness and falsehood, than of a God desirous to preserve, enlighten, and beautify mankind.

CHAP. XI.

OF CHRISTIAN MORALITY.

WERE we to believe Christians, there could have been no true morality on earth, before the coming, of the founder of their sect. They represent the world as having been plunged in darkness and vice at all times and places where Christ was unknown. Yet morality was always necessary to mankind; for, without it, no society can exist. We find, that before the time of Christ, there were flourishing and virtuous nations, and enlightened philosophers, who continually reminded mankind of their duties. The precepts of Socrates, Confucius, and the Gymnosophists of India, are by no means inferior to those of the Messiah of the Christians. We find, amongst heathens, innumerable instances of equity, humanity, temperance, disinterestedness, patience, and meekness, which flatly contradict the pretensions of the Christians, and prove that, before Christ was known on earth, virtues flourished, which were far more real than those he came to teach to men.

Was a supernatural revelation necessary to inform mankind that society cannot exist without virtue, and that, by the admission of vice, societies consent to their own destruction? Was it necessary that a God should speak, to shew that they have need of mutual aid and mutual love ? Was assistance from on High necessary to discover that revenge is an evil, and an outrage upon the laws, which, when they are just, assume to themselves the right of retribution? Is not the forgiveness of injuries connected with this principle? And is not hatred eternalized where implacable revenge is exercised? Is not the pardoning of our enemies a greatness of soul, which gives us an advantage over those who offend us? When we do good to our enemies does it not give us a superiority over them? Is not such conduct calculated to multiply our friends? Does not every man, who is desirous to live, perceive that vice, intemperance, and voluptuousness must shorten the period of life? Has not experience demonstrated to every thinking being that vice is injurious and detestable, even to those who are not free from its empire, and that the practice of virtue is the only means of acquiring real esteem and love? However little mankind may reflect on what they themselves, their true interests, and the end of society are, they must feel what they ought to be to each other. Good laws will render them good; and where these exist, there is no need of flying to heaven for rules for the preservation and happiness of society. Reason is sufficient to teach us our duties to our fellow-creatures. What assistance can it receive from a religion by which it is continually contradicted and degraded?

It is said, that Christianity, far from counteracting morality, is its chief support, and renders its obligations more sacred, by giving them the sanction of God. In my opinion, however, the Christian religion, instead of supporting morality renders it weak and precarious. It cannot possibly have any solid foundation on the commands of a God, who is changing, partial and capricious; and ordains with the same mouth, justice and injustice, concord and carriage, toleration and persecution. It is impossible to follow the precepts of a rational morality, under the empire of a religion, which makes a merit of the most destructive zeal, enthusiasm, and fanaticism. A religion, which commands us to imitate the conduct of a despot who delights to ensnare his creatures, who is implacable in his vengeance, and devotes to flaming destruction all who have the misfortune to displease him, is incompatible with all morality. The innumerable crimes with which the Christian, more than any other religion, has stained itself, have always been committed under the pretext of pleasing the ferocious God whom the Christians have inherited from the Jews. The moral character of this God, must, of necessity, govern the moral conduct of those who adore him.

Hence arises the uncertainty or Christians, whether it be most conformable to the spirit of their religion to *tolerate*, or to *persecute*, those who differ from them in opinion. The two parties find themselves equally authorised in modes of conduct which are diametrically opposite. At one time, Jehovah declares his detestation of idolators, and makes it a duty to exterminate them; at another time Moses forbids his people to *speak ill of the God of nations*. The Son of God forbids persecution, after having said that men must be constrained to enter into his kingdom. Yet, as the idea of a severe and cruel God makes a much deeper impression than that of a bounteous one, true Christians have generally thought it their duty to exert their zeal against those whom they have supposed to be enemies to their God. They have imagined it impossible to offend him by espousing his cause with too much ardour. Toleration has seldom been practised, except by indolent and phlegmatic Christians, of a temperament little analogous to that of the God whom they serve.

Must not a true Christian, to whose imitation the examples of the saints and heroes of the Old Testament are proposed, become ferocious and sanguinary? Will he not find motives for cruelty in the conduct of Moses, who twice caused the blood of Israel to stream, and immolated to his God more than forty thousand victims? To justify his own, will he not appeal to the perfidious cruelty of Phineas, Jabel, and Judith? Will he not see David to be a monster of barbarity, adultery, and rebellion, which nevertheless does not prevent his being a *man after God's own heart*? In short, the whole Bible informs the Christian that his God is delighted with a furious zeal in his service; and this zeal is sufficient to close his eyes on every species of crime.

Let us not then, be surprised to see Christians incessantly persecuting each other. If they are at any time tolerant, it is only when they are themselves persecuted, or too weak to persecute others. Whenever they have power they become the terror and destruction of each other. Since Christianity first appeared on earth, its different sects have incessantly quarrelled. They have mutually exercised the most refined cruelty. Sovereigns, in imitation of David, have espoused the quarrels of discordant priests, and served God by fire and sword. Kings themselves have often perished the victims of religious fanaticism, which tramples on every moral duty in obedience to its God.

In a word, the religion, which boasts of having brought peace on earth, and good will towards men, has for eighteen centuries caused more ravages, and greater effusions of blood, than all the superstitions of heathenism. It has raised walls of separation between the citizens of the same state. It has abandoned concord and affection from families. It has made a duty of injustice and inhumanity. The followers of a God, who was unjustly offended at mankind, became as unjust as he. The servants of a jealous and vindictive God, conceived it their duty to enter into his quarrels and avenge his injuries. Under a God of cruelty, it was judged meritorious to cause the earth to echo with groans, and float in blood.

Such are the important services which the Christian religion has rendered to morality. Let it not be said, that it is through a shameful abuse of this religion, that these horrors have happened. A spirit of persecution and intolerance is the spirit of a religion ordained by a God, jealous of his power, a God who has formally commanded the commission of murder; a God, who, in the excess of his anger, has not spared even his own Son! The servant of such a God is much surer to please him by exterminating his enemies, than by permitting them to offend him in peace. Such a God must necessarily serve as a pretext to the most destructive excesses. A zeal for his glory is used as a veil to conceal the passions of all impostors and fanatics who pretend to be interpreters of the will of heaven; and the enthusiastic hopes to wash away the greatest crimes by bathing his bands in the blood of the enemies of his God.

By a natural consequence of the same principles, an intolerant religion can be only conditionally submissive to the authority of temporal sovereigns. Jews and Christians cannot be obedient to a temporal government, unless its laws be conformed to the arbitrary and often ridiculous commands of their God. But who shall decide whether the laws, most advantageous to society, are conformed to the will of this God? Without doubt, has ministers, the confidants of his secrets and interpreters of his oracles. Thus, in a Christian state, the citizens must be subject rather to spiritual than temporal government, to the priest rather than the magistrate. Hence must arise civil war, bloodshed, proscription, and all that inspires the human breast with horror.

Such is the support afforded to morality by a religion, the first principle of which is to admit the God of the Jews, that is, a tyrant, whose fantastic commands annihilate every rule necessary to the tranquil existence of society. This God creates justice and injustice, his supreme will changes good into bad, and vice into virtue. His caprice overturns the laws which he himself had given to nature. He destroys at his pleasure the moral relations among mankind. In his own conduct he dispenses with all duties towards his creatures. He seems to authorise them to follow no certain laws, except those prescribed to them, in different circumstances, by the voice of his ministers and prophets. These, when in power, preach nothing but submission. If an attempt be made to abridge that power, they preach arms and rebellion. Are they weak? They preach toleration, patience, and meekness. Are they strong? They preach persecution, revenge, rapine, and cruelty. They always find in Holy Writ arguments to authorise these different modes of conduct. They find in the oracles of their just and immutable God, arguments amply sufficient to justify actions diametrically opposite in their nature and offence. To lay the foundation of morality on such a God, or open books which contain laws so contradictory, is to give it an unstable base; it is to found it on the caprice of those who speak in the name of God; it is to found it on the temperament of each one of his adorers.

Morality should be founded upon invariable rules. A God who destroys these rules destroys his own work. If God be the creator of man, if he intends their happiness and preservation, he would have them to be just, humane, and benevolent, and averse to injustice, fanaticism, and cruelty.

From what has been said, we may see what we ought to think of those divines who pretend that, without the Christian religion there could be neither morality nor virtue among mankind. The converse of this proposition would much nigher approach the truth; and it might be maintained, that every Christian who imitates his God, and practises all his commands, must necessarily be an immoral person. If it be said, that those commands are not always unjust, and that the scriptures often breathe benevolence, harmony, and equity, I answer, Christians must have an inconstant morality, sometimes good and sometimes bad, according to interest and individuals. It appears that Christians must either be wholly destitute of true morality, or vibrate continually from virtue to vice, and from vice to virtue.

The Christian religion is but a rotten prop to morality. It will not bear examination, and every man who discovers as defects will be ready to believe that the morality founded on such a basis can be only a chimera. Thus we often behold men, who have couched the neck beneath the yoke of religion, break loose at once and abandon themselves to debauchery, intemperance, and every kind of vice. Escaping from the slavery of superstition, they fly to complete anarchy, and disbelieve the existence of all moral duties, because they have found religion to be but a fable. Hence, among Christians, the words infidel and libertine have become synonymous. All these inconveniencies would be avoided, if mankind, instead of being taught a theological, were taught a natural morality. Instead of interdicting intemperance and vice, because they are offensive to God and religion, they should be prevented, by convincing man that they are destructive to his existence, and render him contemptible in society: that they are disapproved and forbidden by reason and nature, who aim at his preservation, and direct him to take the path that leads to permanent felicity. Whatever may be the will of God, and independently of the future reward, and punishments announced by religion, it is easy to prove to every man that it is, in this world, his interest to preserve his health, to respect virtue, acquire the esteem of his fellow-creatures, and, in fine, to be chaste, temperate, and virtuous. Those whose passions will not suffer them to attend to principles so clear and reasonable, will not be more docile to the voice of a religion, which they will cease to believe the moment it opposes their misguiding propensities.

Let, then, the pretended advantages which the Christian religion lends morality be no longer boasted. The principles drawn from revelation tend to its destruction. We have frequent examples of Christian nations, whose morals are far more corrupted than those of people whom they style infidels and heathens. The former are, at least, most subject to religious fanaticism, a passion calculated to banish justice and all the social virtue from society.

Christianity creates intolerants and persecutors, who are much more injurious to society than the most abandoned debauchees. It is, at least, certain, that the most Christian nations of Europe, are not those where true morality is most felt and practised. In Spain, Portugal, and Italy, where the most superstitious sect of Christians has fixed its residence, people live in the most shameful ignorance of their duties. Robbery, assassination, debauchery, and persecution, are there carried to their worst extreme; and yet all men are full of religion. Few virtuous men exist in those countries. Religion itself there becomes an accomplice to vice, furnishes criminals with an asylum, and procures to them easy means of reconciliation with God. Presents, prayers, and ceremonies, there furnish mankind with a dispensation from the practice of virtue. Amongst nations, who boast of possessing Christianity in all its purity, religion has so entirely absorbed the attention of its sectaries, that morality enters not into their thought; and they think they fulfil all their duties by a scrupulous observation of the minutiae of superstitious ceremonies, whilst they are strangers to all social affections, and labour for the destruction of human happiness.

CHAP. XII.

OF THE CHRISTIAN VIRTUES.

WHAT has been said is sufficient to show what we ought to think of Christian morality. If we examine the virtues recommended in the Christian religion, we find them but ill calculated for mankind. They lift him above his sphere, are useless to society, and often of dangerous consequence. In the boasted precepts, which Jesus Christ came to give mankind, we find little but extravagant maxims, the practice of which is impossible, and rules which, literally followed, must prove injurious to society. In those of his precepts that are practicable, we find nothing which was not as well or better known to the sages of antiquity, without the aid of revelation.

According to the Messiah, the whole duty of man consists in loving God above all things, and his neighbour as himself. Is it possible to obey this precept? Can man love a God above all things, who is represented as wrathful, capricious, unjust, and implacable? who is said to he cruel enough to damn his creatures eternally? Can man love, above all things, an object the most dreadful that human imagination could ever conceive? Can such an object excite in the human heart a sentiment of love? How can we love that which we dread? How can we delight in the God under whose rod we tremble? Do we not deceive ourselves when we think we love a being so terrible, and so calculated to excite nothing but horror?[28]

Is it even practicable for mankind to love their neighbours as themselves? Every man naturally loves himself in preference to all others. He loves his fellow creatures only in proportion as they contribute to his happiness. He exercises virtue in doing good to his neighbour. He acts generously when he sacrifices his self love to his love for another. Yet he will never love his fellow creatures

---

[28] Seneca says, with much truth, that a man of sense cannot fear the Gods, because no man can love what he fears. De Benef. 4. The Bible says, the fear of the Lord is the beginning of wisdom. I think it rather the beginning of folly.

but for the useful qualities he finds in them. He can love them no farther than they are known to him, and his love for them must ever be governed by the good he receives from them.

To love one's enemies is then impossible. A man may abstain from doing evil to the person by whom he is injured; but love is an affection which can he excited in our hearts only by an object which we supposed friendly to us. Politic nations, who have enacted just and wise laws, have always forbidden individuals to revenge, or do justice to themselves. A sentiment of generosity, of greatness of soul or heroism, may induce mankind to do good to those from whom they suffer injuries. By such means they exalt themselves above their enemies, and may even change the disposition of their hearts. Thus, without having recourse to a supernatural morality, we feel that it is our interest to stifle in our hearts the lust of revenge. Christians may, therefore, cease to boast the forgiveness of injuries, as a precept that could be given only by their God, and which proves the divine origin of their morality. Pythagoras, long before the time of Christ, had said, let men revenge themselves upon their enemies, only by labouring to convert them into friends. Socrates taught that it was not lawful for a man, who had received an injury, to revenge it by doing another injury.

Christ must have forgotten that he spoke to men, when, in order to conduct them to perfection, he commanded them to abandon their possessions to the avidity of the first who should demand them; to turn the other check to receive a new insult; to oppose no resistance to the most outrageous violence; to renounce the perishable riches of this world; to forsake houses, possessions, relations, and friends to follow him; and to reject even the most innocent pleasures. Who does not see, in these sublime precepts, the language of enthusiasm and hyperbole? Are not they calculated to discourage man, and throw him into despair? If literally practised, would they not prove ruinous to society?

What shall we say of the morality, which commands the human heart to detach itself from objects which reason commands it to love? When we refuse the blessings offered us by nature, do we not despise the benefactions of the One Supreme? What real good can result to society front the melancholy and ferocious virtues which Christians consider indispensable? Can a man continue useful to society, when his mind is perpetually agitated with imaginary terrors, gloomy ideas, and black inquietudes, which incapacitate him for the performance of his duties to his family, his country, and mankind? If the Christian adhere strictly to the gloomy principles of his religion, must he not become equally insupportable to himself, and those by whom he is surrounded?

It cannot be said, that, in general, fanaticism and enthusiasm are the bases of the morality of Christ. The virtues which he recommends tend to render men unsocial, to plunge them into melancholy, and often to render them injurious to their fellow-creatures. Among human beings, human virtues are necessary; Christian virtues are not calculated on the scale of real life. Society has need of real virtues, from which it may derive energy, activity, and support. Vigilance, labour, and affection, are necessary to families. A desire of enjoying lawful pleasures, and augmenting the sum of their happiness, is necessary to all mankind. The Christian religion is perpetually busied in degrading mankind by threatening them with dismaying terrors, or diverting them with frivolous hopes; sentiments equally proper to turn them from their true duties. If the Christian literally obey the precepts of his legislator, he will ever be either an useless or injurious member of society. [29]

---

[29] Notwithstanding the eulogies lavished by Christians on the precepts of their divine master, same of them are wholly contrary to equity and right reason. When Jesus says, make to yourselves friends in heaven with the mammon of unrighteousness, does he not plainly insinuate, that we may take from others wherewithal to give aims to the poor? Divines will say that he spoke in parables; these parables are, however, easily unfolded. In the mean time, this precept is but too well followed. Many Christians cheat and swindle during all their lives, to have the pleasure of making donations at their death to churches, monasteries, &c. The Messiah at another time, treated his mother, who with parental solicitude was seeking him, extremely ill. He commands his disciples

What real advantage can mankind derive from those ideal virtues, which Christians style evangelic, divine, &.c. and which they prefer to the social, humane, and substantial virtues, and without which they pretend no man can please God, or enter into his glory? Let us examine those boasted virtues in detail. Let us see of what utility they are to society, and whether they truly merit the preference which is given them, to those which are pointed out by reason, as necessary to the welfare of mankind.

The first of the Christian virtues is faith, which serves as a foundation for all the others. It consists in an impossible conviction of the revealed doctrines and absurd fables which the Christian religion commands its disciples to believe. Hence it appears that this virtue exacts a total renunciation of reason, and impracticable assent to improbable facts, and a blind submission to the authority of priests, who are the only guarantees of the truth of the doctrines and miracles that every Christian must believe under penalty of damnation.

This virtue, although necessary to all mankind, is, nevertheless, a gift of heaven, and the effect of a special grace. It forbids all doubt and enquiry; and it deprives man of the liberty of exercising his reason and reflection. It reduces him to the passive acquiescence of beasts in matters which he is, at the same time, told are of all, things the most important to his happiness. Hence it is plain, that faith is a virtue invented by men, who, shrinking from the light of reason, deceived their fellow-creatures, to subject them to their own authority, and degraded them that they might exercise an empire over them. If faith be a virtue, it is certainly useful only to the spiritual guides of the Christians, for they alone gather its fruits. It cannot but be injurious to other men, who are taught by it to despise that reason, which distinguishes them from brutes, and is their only faithful guide in this world. Christians, however, represent this reason as perverted, and an unfaithful guide; by which they seem to intimate that it

---

to steal an ass. He drowns an herd of swine, &c. It must be confessed, these things do not agree extremely well with good morality.

was not made for reasonable beings. May we not, however, ask them how far this renunciation of reason ought to be carried? Do not they themselves, in certain cases, have recourse to reason? Do they not appeal to reason, when they endeavour to prove the existence of their God?

Be this as it may, it is all absurdity to say we believe that of which we have no conception. What, then, are the motives of the Christian, for pretending to such a belief? His confidence in his spiritual guides. But what is the foundation of this confidence? Revelation. On what, then, is Revelation itself founded? On the authority of spiritual guides. Such is the manner in which Christians reason. Their arguments in favour of faith are comprised in the following sentence. To believe our religion it is necessary to have faith, and to have faith you must believe in our religion. Or, it is necessary to have faith already, in order to believe in the necessity of faith[30].

The phantom Faith vanishes at the approach of the sun of reason. It can never sustain a calm examination. Hence it arises that certain Christian divines are so much at enmity with science. The founder of their religion declared, that his law was made for ignorant men and children. Faith is the effect of a grace which God seldom grants to enlightened persons, who are accustomed to consult their reason. It is adapted only to the minds of men who are incapable of reflection, rendered insane by enthusiasm, or invincibly attached to the prejudices of childhood. Science must ever be at enmity with this religion; for in proportion as either of them gains ground the other must lose.

---

[30] Many divines have maintained, that faith without works is sufficient for salvation. This is the virtue which is, in general, most cried up by them. It is, at least, the one most necessary to their existence. It is not, therefore, surprising that they have endeavoured to establish it by fire and sword. It was for the support of faith that the Inquisition burned heretics and Jews. Kings and priests persecute for the establishment of faith. Christians have destroyed those who were destitute of faith, in order to demonstrate to them their error. O wondrous virtue, and worthy of the God of mercies! His ministers punish mankind, when he refuses them his grace!!!

Another Christian virtue, proceeding from the former, is Hope. Founded on the flattering promises given by this religion to those who render themselves wretched in this life, it feeds their enthusiasm. It induces them firmly to believe that God will reward, in heaven, their gloominess. inutility, indolence, prayers, and detestation of pleasures on earth. How can a man, who, being intoxicated with these pompous hopes, becomes indifferent to his own happiness, concern himself with that of his fellow-creatures? The Christian believes that he pleases his God by rendering himself miserable in this life ; and however flattering his hopes may be for the future, they are here empoisoned by the idea of a jealous God, who commands him to work out his own salvation with fear and trembling, and who will plunge him into eternal torture, if he for a moment has the weakness to be a man.

Another of the Christian virtues is Charity. It consists in loving God and our neighbour. We have always seen how difficult, not to say impossible, it is to feel sentiments of tenderness for any being whom we fear. It will, undoubtedly be said, that the fear of Christians is a filial fear. But words cannot change the essence of things. Fear is a passion, totally opposite to love. A son, who rears the anger, and dreads the caprices of a father, can never love him sincerely. The love, therefore, of a Christian to his God can never he true. In vain he endeavours to feel sentiments of tenderness for a rigorous master, at whose idea his heart shrinks back in terror. He can never love him but as a tyrant, to whom his mouth renders the homage that his heart refuses. The devotee is not honest to himself, when he pretends to love his God. His affection is a dissembled homage, like that which men are forced to render to certain inhuman despots, who, while they tread their subjects in the dust, demand from them the exterior marks of attachment. If some tender minds, by force of illusion, feel sentiments or divine love, it is then a mystic and romantic passion, produced by a warm temperament, and an ardent imagination, which present their God to them dressed in smiles, with all his imputed faults concealed.[31] The love of God is not the least incomprehensible mystery of this religion.

Charity, considered as the love of mankind, is a virtuous and necessary disposition. It then becomes no more than that tender humanity which attaches us to our fellows, and inclines us to love and assist them. But how shall we reconcile this attachment with the commands of a jealous God, who would have us to love none but himself, and who came to separate the friend from the friend, and the son from the father? According to the precepts of the gospel, it would be criminal to offer God a heart shared by an earthly object. It would be idolatry thus to confound the creature with the Creator. And further, how can the Christian love beings who continually offend his God? Beings who would continually betray himself into offence? How can he love sinners? Experience teaches us that the devout, obliged by principle to hate themselves, have very little more affection for others. If this be not the case, they have not arrived at the perfection of divine love. We do not find that those, who are so supposed to love the Creator most ardently, show much affection for his creatures. On the contrary, we see them fill with bitterness all who surround them; they criticise with severity the faults of others, and make it a crime to speak of human frailty with indulgence.[32] A sincere love for God must be accompanied with zeal,

---

[31] It is an ardent and tender temperament that produces mystic devotion. Hysterical women are those who commonly love God with most vivacity, they love him to distraction, as they would love a man. In monasteries, particularly Ste. Madeleine de Pazzy, Marie a la Coque, most of the devotees are of this description. Their imagination grows wild, and they give to their God, whom they paint in the most captivating colours, that tenderness which they are not permitted to bestow on beings of their own species. It requires a strong imagination to be smitten with an object unknown.

[32] Devotees are generally considered as scourges of society. A devout woman has seldom the talent of conciliating the love of her husband and his domestics. A gloomy and melancholy religion cannot render its disciples very amiable. A sad and sullen monarch must have sad and sullen subjects. Christians have judiciously remarked, that Jesus Christ wept, but never smiled.

A true Christian must be enraged when he sees his God offended. He must arm himself with a just and holy severity to repress the offenders. He must have an ardent desire to extend the empire of his religion. A zeal, originating in this divine love, has been the source of the terrible persecutions of which Christians have so often been guilty. Zeal produces murderers as well as martyrs. It is zeal that prompts intolerant man to wrest the thunder from the hand of the Most High, to avenge him of his enemies. It is this that causes members of the same state, and the same family, to detest and torment each other for opinions, and puerile ceremonies, which they are led to esteem as of the last importance. It is this zeal that has a thousand times kindled those religious wars so remarkable for their atrocity. Finally, it is this zeal for religion which justifies calumny, treason, carnage, and, in short, the disorders most fatal to society. It has always been considered as lawful to employ artifice, falsehood, and force, in support of the cause of God. The most choleric and corrupted men are commonly the most zealous. They hope that, for the sake of their zeal, Heaven will pardon the depravity of their manners be it ever so excessive.

It is from an effect of the same zeal that enthusiastic Christians fly over every sea and continent to extend the empire of their God and make new proselytes. Stimulated by this zeal, missionaries go to trouble the repose of what they call heathen nations, whilst they would be astonished and enraged to find missionaries from those nations endeavouring to propagate a new religion in their country. [33]

When these propagators of the faith have had power in their hands, they have excited the most horrid rebellions; and have, in conquered countries, exercised cruelties calculated only to render the God detestable whom they pretended to serve. They have thought that men who have so long been strangers to their God

---

[33] Kambi, Emperor of China, asked the Jesuit missionaries at Pekin, what they would say, if he should send missionaries to their nation. The revolts excited by Jesuits in Japan and Ethiopia are well known. A holy missionary has been heard to say, that without muskets, missionaries could never make proselytes.

could be little better than beasts; and, therefore, judged it lawful to exercise every kind of violence over them. In the eyes of a Christian an infidel is seldom worthier than a dog.

It is apparently in imitation of the Jews that Christian nations have usurped the possessions of the inhabitants of the new world. The Castilians and Portuguese had the same right to the possession of America and Africa, that the Hebrews had to make themselves masters of the land of Canaan, and exterminate its inhabitants, or reduce them to slavery. Have not Popes arrogated the right of disposing of distant empires to their favourite Monarchs in Europe? These manifest violations of the law of nature and of nations appeared just to those Christian Princes, in favour of whom religion sanctified avarice, cruelty, and usurpation. [34]

Humility is, also, considered by Christians as a sublime virtue, and of inestimable value. No supernatural and divine revelations are necessary to teach us that pride does not become man, and that it renders him disagreeable to others. All must be convinced, on a moment's reflection, that arrogance, presumption, and vanity, are disgusting and contemptible qualities. But Christian humility is carried to a more refined extreme. The Christian must renounce his reason, mistrust his virtues, refuse to do justice to his own good actions,, and repress all self-esteem, however well merited. Whence it appears, that this pretended virtue only degrades and debases man in his own eyes, deprives him of all energy, and stifles in him every desire of rendering himself useful to society. To forbid mankind to esteem themselves and merit the esteem of others, as to break the only powerful string that inclines them to study, industry, and noble

---

[34] St. Augustin says, that of right divine, all things belong to the just. A maxim which is founded on a passage in the Psalms, which says, the just shall eat the fruit of the labour of the unrighteous. It is known that the Pope, by a bull given in favour of the kings of Castile, Arragon, and Portugal, fixed the line of demarcation which was to rule the conquests which each had gained over the Infidels. After such principles, is not the whole earth to become a prey to Christian rapacity?

actions. This Christian virtue is calculated only to render them abject slaves, wholly useless to the world, and make all virtue give place in them to a blind submission to their spiritual guides.

Let us not be surprised, that a religion which boasts of being supernatural should endeavour to unnaturalize man. This religion, in the delirium of its enthusiasm, forbids mankind to love themselves. It commands them to hate pleasures and court grief. It makes a merit of all voluntary evils they do unto themselves. Hence those austerities and penances so destructive to health; those extravagant mortifications, cruel privations, and gradual suicides, by which fanatic Christians think they merit heaven. It must be confessed, all Christians do not feel themselves capable of such marvellous perfections, but all believe themselves more or less obliged to mortify the flesh, and renounce the blessings prepared for them by a bounteous God, who they suppose, offers his good things only that they may be refused, and would be offended should his creatures presume to touch them.

Reason cannot approve virtues which are destructive to ourselves, nor admit a God who is delighted when mankind render themselves miserable, and voluntarily submit to torments. Reason and experience, without the aid of superstition, are sufficient to prove, that passions and pleasures, pushed to excess, destroy us; and that the abuse of the best things becomes a real evil. Nature herself inculcates upon us the privation of things which prove injurious to us. A being, solicitous for his own preservation, must restrain irregular propensities, and fly whatever tends to his destruction. It is plain, that by the Christian religion, suicide is, at least, indirectly authorised.

It was in consequence of these fanatical ideas that, in the earliest ages of Christianity, the forests and deserts were peopled with perfect Christians, who by flying from the world, left their families destitute of support, and their country of citizens, to abandon themselves to an idle and contemplative life. Hence those legions of monks and cenobites, who, under the standards of different enthusiasts, have enrolled themselves into a militia, burthensome and injurious to society. They thought to merit heaven, by burying talents, which might be serviceable to their fellow-citizens, and vowing a life of indolence and celibacy. Thus, in nations which are the most faithful to Christianity, a multitude of men render themselves useless and wretched all their lives. What heart is so hard as to refuse a tear to the lot of the hapless victims taken from that enchanting sex which was destined to give happiness to our own! Unfortunate dupes of youthful enthusiasm, or sacrificed to the ambitious views of imperious families, they are for ever exiled from the world! They are bound by rash oaths to unending slavery and misery. Engagements, contradicted by every precept of nature, force them to perpetual virginity. It is in vain that riper feelings, sooner or later, warm their breasts, and make them groan under the weight of their imprudent vows. They regret their voluntary sterility, and find themselves forgotten in society. Cut off from their families, and subjected to troublesome and despotic gaolers, they sink into a life of disgust, of bitterness, and tears. In fine, thus exiled from society, thus unrelated and unbeloved, there only remains for them the shocking consolation of seducing other victims to share with them the torments of their solitude and mortifications.

The Christian religion seems to have undertaken to combat nature and reason in every thing. If it admits some virtues, approved by reason, it always carries them to a vicious excess. It never observes that just mean, which is the point of perfection. All illicit and shameful pleasures will be avoided by every man, who is desirous of his own preservation, and the esteem of his fellow-creatures. The heathens knew and taught this truth, notwithstanding the depravity of morals with which they are reproached by Christians.[35] The church even recommends celibacy

---

[35] Aristotle and Epictetus recommended chastity of speech. Manander said, that a good man could never consent to debauch a virgin or commit adultery. Tibullus said, casta placent superis. Mark Anthony thanks the Gods, that he had preserved his chastity in his youth. The Romans made laws against adultery. Father Tachard informs us, that the Siamans forbid not only dishonest actions, but also impure thoughts and desires. Whence it appears, that chastity and purity of manners were esteemed even before the Christian religion existed.

as a state of perfection, and considers the natural tie of marriage as an approach to sin. God, however, declares in Genesis, that it is not good for man to be alone. He also formally commanded all creatures to increase and multiply. His Son, in the gospel, comes to annul those laws. He teaches that, to attain to perfection, it is necessary to avoid marriage, and resist the strongest desire with which the breast of man is inspired--that of perpetuating his existence by a posterity, and providing supports for his old age and infirmities.

If we consult reason, we find, that the pleasures of love are always injurious when taken in excess; and that they are always criminal when they prove injurious. We shall perceive, that to debauch a woman is to condemn her to distress and infamy, and annihilate to her all the advantages of society; that adultery is destructive to the greatest felicity of human life, conjugal union. Hence we shall be convinced, that marriage, being the only means, of satisfying our desire of increasing the species and providing filial supports, is a state far more respectable and sacred, than the destructive celibacy and voluntary castration recommended as a virtue by the Christian religion.

Nature, or its author, invites man, by the attraction of pleasure, to multiply himself. He has unequivocally declared, that women are necessary to men. Experience shows, that they are formed for society, not solely for the purpose of a transient pleasure, but to give mutual assistance in the misfortunes of life, to produce and educate children, form them into citizens, and provide in them support for themselves in old age. In giving man superior strength, nature has pointed out his duty of labouring for the support of his family; the weaker organs of his companion are destined to functions less violent, but not less necessary. In giving her a soul more soft and sensible, nature has, by a tender sentiment, attached her more particularly to her children. Such are the sure bands which the Christian religion would tear asunder. Such the blessings it would wrest from man, while it substitutes in their place an unnatural celibacy, which renders man selfish and useless, depopulates society, and which can be advantageous only to the odious policy of some Christian priests, who, separating from their fellow-citizens, have formed a destructive body, which eternalizes itself without posterity. *Gens aeterna in qua nemo nascitur.*

If this religion has permitted marriage to some sects, who have not the temerity to soar to the highest pinnacle of perfection, it seems to have sufficiently punished them for this indulgence, by the unnatural shackles it has fixed on the connubial state. Thus, among them, we see divorce forbidden, and the most wretched unions indissoluble. Persons once married, are forced to groan under the weight of wedlock, even when affection and esteem are dead, and the place of these essentials to conjugal happiness is supplied by hatred and contempt. Temporal laws also conspiring with religion, forbid the wretched prisoners to break their chains. It seems as if the Christian religion exerted all its powers to make us view marriage with disgust, and give the preference to a celibacy which is pregnant with debauchery, adultery, and dissolution. Yet the God of the Hebrews made divorce lawful, and I know not by what right his Son, who came to accomplish the law of Moses, revoked an indulgence so reasonable.

Such are the perfections which Christianity inculcates on her children, and such the virtues she prefers to those which are contemptuously styled human virtues. She even rejects these, and calls them false and sinful, because their possessors are, forsooth, not filled with faith. What! the virtues of Greece and Rome, so amiable, and so heroic, were they not true virtues? If justice, humanity, generosity, temperance, and patience be not virtues, to what can the name be given? And are the virtues less because professed by heathens? Are not the virtues of Socrates, Cato, Epictetus, and Antonine, real and preferable to the zeal of the Cyrills, the obstinacy of Athanasius, the uselessness of Anthony, the rebellion of Chrysostom, the ferocity of Dominic, and the meanness of Francis?

All the virtues admitted by Christians, are either overstrained and fanatic, tending to render man useless, abject, and miserable, or obstinate, haughty, cruel, and destructive to society. Such are the effects of a religion, which contemning the earth, hesitates not to overwhelm it with trouble, provided it thereby heightens the triumph of its God over his enemies. No true morality can ever be compatible with such a religion.

CHAP. XIII.

OF THE PRACTICE AND DUTIES OF THE CHRISTIAN RELIGION.

IF the Christian virtues be destitute or solidity, and produce no effect which reason can approve, we shall find nothing more estimable in a multitude of incommodious, useless, and often dangerous practices, which Christians consider as their sacred duties, and by means of which they are confident of obtaining the pardon and favours of God, and an eternal abode with him in unspeakable glory and felicity.

The first and most essential duty of Christians is prayer. To continual prayer their religion attaches its felicity. Their God, whom they suppose to be overflowing with bounty, refuses to bestow his blessings unsolicited. He grants them only to importunity. Sensible to flattery, like the kings of the earth, he exacts an etiquette, and bears no petitions unless they are presented in a certain form. What should we say of a father who, knowing the wants of his children, should refuse to give them necessary food, until wearied out with fervent supplications? But in another view, does it imply mistrust of the wisdom of God to prescribe rules for his conduct? Does it not imply a doubt of his immutability, to believe he can be prevailed on by his creatures to alter his designs? If he knows all things, what need is there of continually informing him what are the dispositions and desires of his subjects? If he is almighty, how can he be flattered with the submissions, adorations, and formalities with which Christians prostrate themselves before him?

In one word, prayer supposes a capricious God, deficient in memory, voracious of praise, fond of seeing his creatures abased in the dust, and anxious to receive at every instant the most abject marks of their submission.

Can these ideas, borrowed from earthly princes, be with propriety applied to an omnipotent Being, who created the universe for man, and desires only that he should be happy? Can it be supposed that such a Being, without equal and without rival, should be jealous of his glory? Can the prayers of man and glory to a Being beyond comparison superior to all others? Cannot Christians see, that, in endeavouring to honour and exalt their God, they only degrade and debase him?

Is also the opinion of Christians, that the prayers of one man may be serviceable to others. Partial to his favourites, God bears petitions only from their lips. He listens not to his people, unless their prayers be offered up to him through his ministers. He becomes a sultan, accessible only to his ministers, visirs, eunuchs, and the women of his Seraglio. Hence the millions of priests and cenobites, who have no business on earth, but to raise their idle hands to heaven, and pray night and day for its blessings to society. Nations pay dearly for these important services, and these pious impostors live in splendour and ease, while real merit, labour, and industry languish in misery.

Under the pretence of devoting himself to prayer and other ceremonies of his worship, the Christian, particularly in some of the more superstitious sects, is obliged to remain idle, and stand with arms across during a great part of the year. He is persuaded that he honours God by his inutility. Feasts and fasts, multiplied by the interests of priests and the credulity of the people, often suspended for long intervals the labours necessary to the subsistence of society. Men fly to temples to pray when they should stay at home and cultivate their fields. There their eyes are fed with childish ceremonies, and their ears are filled with fables and doctrines, of which they can comprehend nothing. This tyrannical religion makes it a crime for the poor labourer to endeavour, during consecrated days, to procure subsistence for a numerous and indigent family. And civil authority, in concert with religion, punishes those who have the audacity to earn bread instead of praying or being idle.

Can reason subscribe to the ridiculous obligation of abstaining from certain aliments and meals which is imposed by some sects of Christians? In consequence of these laws, people, who live by their labour, are forced to content themselves, during long intervals, with dear and unwholesome provisions, more proper to generate disease than repair strength.

What abject and ridiculous ideas must they entertain of God, who believe he can be offended by the quality of the food that enters into the stomachs of his creatures! Heaven, however, for a certain sum of money becomes sometimes more accommodating. Priests have been continually busied in straitening the path of their sectaries, that they might transgress more frequently; and that the revenue arising from their transgressions might thus become more ample. All things, even sin itself, among Christians, contribute to the profit of the priests.

No religion ever placed its sectaries in more complete and continual dependance on priests, than the Christian. Those harpies never lose sight of their prey. They take infallible measures for subjecting mankind, and making all contribute to their power, riches, and dominion. Having assumed the office of mediator between the heavenly monarch and his subjects, these priests were looked upon as courtiers in favour, ministers commissioned to exercise power in his name, and favourites to whom he could refuse nothing. Thus they became absolute masters of the destiny of the Christians. They gained establishments and rendered themselves necessary by the introduction of innumerable practices and duties, which, though puerile and ridiculous, they had the address to make their flocks look upon as indispensibly necessary to their salvation. They represented the omission of these pretended duties as a crime infinitely greater than an open violation of all the laws of morality and reason.

Let us not then be surprized, that, in the most zealous, that is to say the most superstitious sects, we see mankind perpetually infested with priests. Scarce are they born, when, under the pretext of washing away original sin, their priests impose on them a mercenary baptism, and pretend to reconcile them with a God whom they have as yet been unable to offend. By means of a few words and magical ceremonies they are thus snatched from the dominion of Satan. From the tenderest infancy their education is frequently entrusted to priests, whose principal care is to instil into them early the prejudices as necessary to the views of the church. Terrors are now introduced into their minds which increase during their whole lives. They are instructed in the fables, absurd doctrines, and incomprehensible mysteries of a marvellous religion. In one word, they are formed into superstitious Christians, and rendered incapable of being useful citizens or enlightened men. Only one thing is represented to them as necessary, which is to be in all things devoutly submissive to his religion. "Be devout," say his teachers, "be blind, despise thy reason, attend to heaven, and neglect earth; this is all thy God demands to conduct thee to eternal felicity."

To maintain the abject and fanatic ideas with which the priest has filled his pupils in their childhood, he commands them to come frequently, and deposit in his bosom their hidden faults, their most secret actions and thoughts. He obliges them to humiliate themselves at his feet, and render homage to his power. He frightens the criminals, and afterwards, if they are judged worthy, he reconciles them to God, who on the command of his ministers remits their sins. The Christian sects that admit this practice, boast of it as extremely useful in regulating the manners and restraining the passions of men; but experience proves, that the countries in which this usage is most faithfully observed, are distinguished rather for the dissolution than the purity of their manners. By such easy expiations they are only emboldened in vice. The lives of Christians are circles of successive offences and confessions. The priesthood reap the profit of this practice by means of which they exercise an absolute dominion over the consciences of mankind. How great must be the power of an order of men, who possess all the secrets of families, can kindle at pleasure the destructive flame of fanaticism, and open or sbut the gates of heaven!

Without the consent of his priests, the Christian cannot participate the knowledge of the mysteries or his religion, from which they have a right to exclude him entirely. This privation, however, he has no great reason to lament. But the anathemas or excommunications of the priests generally do a real mischief to mankind. These spiritual punishments produce temporal effects, and every citizen who incurs the disgrace of the church is in danger of that of the government, and becomes odious to his fellow-citizens.

We have already remarked that priests have taken upon themselves the management of marriages. Without their consent, a Christian cannot become a father. He must first submit to the capricious formalities of his religion, without which his children must be excluded from the rank of citizens.

During all his life, the Christian is obliged to assist in the ceremonies of worship under the direction of his priests. When he has performed this important duty, he esteems himself the favourite of God, and persuades himself that he no longer owes any thing to society. Thus frivolous practices take place of morality, which is always rendered subordinate to religion.

When death approaches, the Christian, stretched in agony on his bed, is still assailed in those distressful moments by priests. In some sects religion seems to have been invented to render the bitter death of man ten thousand times more bitter. A malicious priest comes to the couch of the dying man, and holds before him the spectacle of his approaching end, arrayed in more than all its terrors. Although this custom is destructive to citizens, it is extremely profitable to the priesthood, [36]who owe much of their riches to legacies procured by it. Morality is not quite so highly advantaged by it. Experience proves, that most Christians live in security and postpone till death their reconciliation with God. By means of a late repentance, and largesses to the priesthood, their faults are expiated, and they are permitted to hope that heaven will forget the accumulated crimes of a long and wicked life.

Death itself does not terminate the empire of the priesthood in certain sects, which finds means to make money even out of the dead bodies of their followers. These, for a sufficient sum, are permitted to be deposited in temples, where they have the

---

[36] In Catholic countries.

privilege of spreading infection and disease. The sacerdotal power extends still further. The prayers of the church are purchased at a dear rate, to deliver the souls of the dead from their pretended torments in the other world, inflicted for their purification. Happy they who are rich, in a religion whose priests, being favourites with God, can be hired to prevail on him to remit the punishments which his immutable justice had intended to inflict.

Such are the principal ditties recommended by the Christians; and upon the observation of these they believe their salvation to depend. Such are the arbitrary, ridiculous, and hurtful practices substituted for the real duties of morality. We shall not combat the different superstitious practices, admitted by some sects and rejected by others; such as the honours rendered to the memory of those pious fanatics and obscure contemplators whom Roman pontiffs have ranked among the saints. We say nothing of those pilgrimages which superstition has so often produced, nor those indulgences by means of which sins are remitted. We shall only observe, that these things are commonly more respected where they are admitted, than the duties of morality, which in those places frequently are wholly unknown. Mankind find their natural propensities much less thwarted by such rites, ceremonies, and practices than by being virtuous. A good Christian is a man who conforms forms exactly to all that his priests exact from him; these substitute blindness and submission in the place of all virtues.

CHAP. XIV.

OF THE POLITICAL EFFECTS OF THE CHRISTIAN RELIGION.

AFTER having seen the inutility and even danger of the perfections, virtues, and duties proposed by the Christian religion, let us enquire whether its political influences be more happy, and whether it can in reality promote the welfare of nations, among whom it is established and faithfully observed. We at once find, that wherever this religion is admitted, two opposite legislations, ever at variance with each other, establish themselves. Although this religion preaches love and peace, it soon annihilates the effects of those precepts by the divisions which it necessarily sows among its sectaries, who unavoidably interpret diversely the ambiguous oracles announced in holy writ. We find, that from the infancy of religion the most acrimonious disputes have continually taken place among divines. The successive ages of Christianity have been stained with schisms, heresies, persecutions, and contests, widely discordant from its boasted spirit of peace and concord; which is in fact incompatible with a religion whose precepts are so dark and equivocal. In all religious disputes, each party believes that God is on its side, and consequently they are obstinate. Indeed, how can it he otherwise, when they confound the cause of God with that of their own vanity? Thus, mutually averse to concession, they quarrel and fight until force has decided a concession, in which they never appeal to reason. In fact, political authorities have ever been forced to interfere, in all the dissensions which have arisen among Christians. Governments have always taken in the frivolous disputes of priests, and foolishly considered them as objects of the last importance. They have conceived that, in a religion established by God himself, there could be nothing of a trifling nature. Thus, princes have arrived themselves against their own subjects, whose opinions differed from theirs. The way of thinking at court has decided the creed and the faith of subjects. Opinions supported by kings and priests have been the only true ones. Their creatures have been the guardians of orthodoxy, and were commissioned to exterminate all whom they chose to denominate heretics and rebels.

The prejudices of princes or their false policy, have caused them to look upon those of their subjects, who differ from themselves in religious opinions, as bad citizens, dangerous to the state, and enemies to their power. If, leaving to priests the business or finishing their own impertinent disputes, they had not assisted their quarrels and persecutions, they would have died away of themselves, and never have disturbed the peace of nations. If those kings had impartially recompensed the good and punished the bad, without regard to their worship, ceremonies, and speculative opinions, they would not have made many of their subjects such enemies to that power, by which they found themselves oppressed. Christians have always attempted to reclaim heretics by injustice, violence, and persecution. Ought not they to have perceived, that this conduct was calculated only to produce hypocrites and hidden enemies, or open rebellions?

But these reflections are not designed for princes, who, from their infancy, have been filled with fanaticism and prejudices. They, instead of being actuated by virtuous motives, have formed obstinate attachments to frivolities, and impetuous ardour for doctrines foreign to the welfare of their states, and a boundless wrath against all who refuse to bend to their despotic opinions. Such sovereigns find it a shorter way to destroy mankind than reclaim them by mild means. Their haughty despotism will not condescend to reason. Religion assures them that tyranny is lawful, and cruelty meritorious when they are employed in the cause of heaven.

The Christian religion, in fact, always makes despots and tyrants of all the sovereigns by whom it is adopted. It represents them as gods upon earth; it causes their very caprices to be respected as the will of heaven itself. It delivers mankind into their hands as an herd of slaves, of whom they may dispose at their pleasure. In return for their zeal for religion, all the outrages upon justice that they can commit are forgiven, and their subjects are commanded, under pain of the wrath of the Most High, to submit without a murmur to the sword that strikes instead of protecting themselves. It is not, therefore, matter of surprise, that since the establishment of this religion, we see so many nations groaning under devout tyrants, who, although obstinately attached to religion, have been unjust, licentious, and cruel. Whatever were the oppressions and ravages of these religious or hypocritical princes, the priests have not failed to preach submission to their subjects. On the other hand, let us not be surprised to see so many weak and wicked princes, support in their turns the interest of a religion, which their false policy judged necessary to the maintenance of their authority. If kings were enlightened, just and virtuous, and knew and practised their real duties, they would have had no need of the aid of superstition in governing nations. But as it is more easy to conform to rites than to acquire talents or practice virtue, this religion has, in princes, too often found support for itself, and destruction for its enemies.

The ministers of religion have not had the same complaisance for princes, who refused to make a common cause with them, espouse their quarrels, and become subservient to their passions. They have arisen against those who have thwarted their views, punished their excesses, touched their immunities, endeavoured to subject them to reason, or repress their ambitious designs. The priests on such occasions, cry out, *Impiety! Sacrilege!* Then they pretend that the sovereign puts his hand to the censor, and usurps the rights granted them by God himself. . Then they endeavour to excite nations to rebellion. They arm fanatics against sovereigns, whom they declare tyrants, for having been wanting in submission to the church. Heaven is always ready to revenge any injustice done to its ministers. They are themselves submissive, and preach submission to others, only when they are permitted to share the authority, or are too feeble to resist it. This is the reason why the apostles, in the infancy of Christianity, being destitute of power, preached subordination. No sooner had this religion gained sufficient strength, than it preached resistance and rebellion; dethroning some kings and assassinating others.

In every political body, where this religion is established, there are two rival powers, which, by incessant contention, convulse and wound the state. The citizens divide into opposite parties, each of which fights, or thinks it fights, for God. These contests at different times terminate differently, but the triumphant party is always in the right. By attentive examination of such events, we shall escape the dominion of fanaticism. It is by stimulating mankind to enquiry, that they must be freed from the shackles of superstition. Let mankind think till they have thrown aside their prejudices, and they will think justly. The reign of the priesthood will cease when men cease to be ignorant and credulous. Credulity is the offspring of ignorance, and superstition is the child of credulity.

But most kings dread that mankind should be enlightened. Accomplices with the priesthood, they have formed a league to stifle reason, and persecute all who confide in its guidance. Blind to their own interests, and those of their subjects, they wish only to command slaves, forgetting those slaves are always at the disposal of the priests. Thus we see science neglected, and ignorance triumphant, in those countries where this religion holds the most absolute dominion. Arts and sciences are the children of liberty, and separated from their parent they languish and die. Among Christian nations, the least superstitious are the most free, powerful, and happy. In countries where spiritual and temporal despotism are leagued, the people grovel in the most shameful ignorance and lethargic inactivity. The European nations, who boast of possessing the purest faith, are not surely the most flourishing and powerful. Their kings, enslaved themselves by priests, have not energy and courage enough to make a single struggle for their own welfare or that of their subjects. Priests, in such states are the only order of men who are rich; other citizens languish in the deepest indigence. But of what importance are the power and happiness of nations to the sectaries of a religion who seek not for happiness in this world, who believe riches injurious, preach a God of poverty, and recommend abasement to the soul, and mortification of the flesh? It is without doubt to oblige people to practise these maxims, that the Clergy, in many Christ states, have taken possession of most of the riches, and live in splendour, while their fellow-citizens are set forward in the road to heaven, unencumbered with any burthen of earthly wealth.

Such are the advantages political society derives from the Christian religion. It forms an independent state within a state. It renders the people slaves. When sovereigns are obedient to it, it favours their tyranny. When they are disobedient, it renders their subjects fanatic and rebellious. When it accords with political power, it convulses, debases, and impoverishes nations; when not, it makes citizens unsocial, turbulent, intolerant, and mutinous.

If we examine in detail the precepts of this religion, and the maxims which flow from its principles, we shall find it interdicts every thing that can make a nation flourish. We have already seen the ideas of imperfection that it attaches to marriage, and its esteem of celibacy. These notions are highly unfavourable to population, which is, incontrovertibly, the first source of power in a state.

Commerce is not less contradictory to the spirit of a religion, the founder of which pronounced an anathema against riches, and excluded them from his kingdom. All industry is interdicted to perfect Christians; they live a provisory life on earth, and never concern themselves with the morrow.

Must it not be a great temerity and sin for a Christian to serve in war? Is not the man, who has never the right to believe himself absolutely in a state of grace, extremely rash when he exposes himself to eternal damnation? Is not the Christian, who ought to have charity with all men, and love even his enemies, guilty of an enormous crime, when he kills a man of whose dispositions he is ignorant, and whom he, perhaps, precipitates at once into hell? A Christian soldier is a monster; unless, indeed, he fights in the cause of religion. Then, if he dies, "he dies a blessed martyr."

The Christian religion has always declared war against science and all human knowledge. These have been looked upon at obstacles to salvation. Neither reason nor study are necessary to men, who are to submit their reason to the yoke of faith. From the confession of Christians themselves, the founders of their religion were simple and ignorant men. Their disciples must be as little enlightened as they were, to admit the fables and reveries they have received from them. It has always been remarked, that the most enlightened men seldom make the best Christians. Science is apt to embarrass faith; and it moreover turns the attention from the great work of salvation, which is represented as the only necessary one. If science be serviceable to political society, ignorance is much more so to religion and its ministers. Those ages, destitute of science and industry, were the golden age of the church of Christ. Then were kings dutifully submissive to priests; then the coffers of priests held all the riches of society. The priests of a very numerous sect have kept from the eyes of their followers even the sacred pages which contain the laws of their religion. This conduct is, undoubtedly, very discreet. Reading the Bible is the surest of all means to prevent its being respected.

In one word, if the maxims of the Christian religion were rigorously and universally followed, no political society could subsist. If this assertion be doubted, listen to what was said by the earliest doctors of the church, and it will be acknowledged, that their precepts are wholly incompatible with the power and preservation of states. According to Lactantius, no Christian can become a soldier. According to St. Justin, no Christian can be a magistrate. According to St. Chrysostom, no Christian can meddle with commerce. And, according to a great number, no man ought to study. In fine, join these maxims to those of Christ, apply them in practice, and the result will be a perfect Christian, useless to his family, his country, and mankind; an idle contemplator, unconcerned in the interests of this world, and occupied entirely with the other, whither it is his most important business to go.

Let us look into Eusebius, and see if the Christian be not a real fanatic, from whom society can derive no advantage. "The manner of life," says he, "in the Christian church, surpasses our present nature, and the ordinary life of man. There they seek neither marriages, children, nor riches. In fact, it is wholly foreign to the human manner of living. The church is given up to an immense love of heavenly things. The members, detached from earthly existence, and leaving only their bodies below, transfer their souls to heaven, where they already dwell as pure and celestial intelligences, and despise the life of other men." A man strongly persuaded of the truth of Christianity cannot, in fact, attach himself to any thing below. Every thing here is to him a cause of stumbling, and calls away his attention from the great work of his salvation. If Christians were not, fortunately, inconsistent with themselves, and wandered not incessantly from their fanatical perfections and sublime speculations, no Christian society could subsist, and the nations illuminated by the gospel would return to their pristine barbarity. We should see only wild beings, broken loose from every social tie, and wandering in solitude through this vale of tears, whose only employment would be, to groan, to weep, and pray, and render themselves and others wretched, in order to merit heaven.

In fine, a religion whose maxims tend to render mankind in general intolerant, to make kings persecutors, and their subjects slaves or rebels; a religion, the obscure doctrines of which give birth to eternal disputes; a religion which debases mankind, and turns them aside from their true interests; such a religion, I say, is destructive to every society.

CHAP. XV.

OF THE CHRISTIAN CHURCH, OR PRIESTHOOD.

THERE have been, in all ages, men who know how to profit by the errors of mankind. Priests of all religions, have laid the foundations of their greatness, power, and riches, on the fears of the vulgar. No religion has, however, had so many reasons as the Christian, for subjecting people to the priesthood. The first preachers of the gospels the Apostles, are represented as divine men, inspired by God, and sharing his omnipotence. If each individual among their successors has not enjoyed the same privileges in the opinion of all Christians, yet the body of priests, or Church, is never abandoned by the Holy Ghost, but always illuminated thereby. They collectively, at all times, possess infallibility, and consequently their decisions become perpetual revelations equally sacred with those or God himself.

Such being the attributes of the priesthood, this body must in virtue of the prerogatives they hold from Christ himself, have a right to unconditional submission from men and nations. The enormous power they have so long exercised is not, therefore, surprising. It should be unlimited, since it is founded on the authority of the Almighty. It should he despotic, because men have no right to resist divine power. It must degenerate into abuse, for the priesthood is exercised by men whom impunity always renders licentious and corrupt.

In the infancy of Christianity, the Apostles, commissioned by Jesus Christ, preached the Gospel to Jews and Gentiles. The novelty of their doctrine, as we have already seen, procured them many proselytes among the vulgar. The new Christians, inflamed with ardour for their new opinions, formed in every city particular congregations, under the government of men appointed by the Apostles. The latter having received the faith at first hand, retained the inspection and direction of the different Christian societies they had formed. Such appears to have been the origin of Bishops or Inspectors, which are perpetuated in the Church to this day;[37] an origin in which the princes of modern Christianity sufficiently pride themselves. It is known that, in this infant sect, the associates held their goods in common. This duty appears to have been rigorously enacted; for, by the command of St. Peter, two new Christians were smitten to death, for having withheld some part of their own property. The funds resulting from this practice, were at the disposal of the Apostles; to this submission the Bishops, Inspectors, or priests succeeded, when they became successors of the Apostles; and as the priests must live by the altar, we may suppose that they paid themselves, and not illiberally, for their instructions, out of the public treasury. Those who attempted new spiritual conquests were, probably, obliged to content themselves with the voluntary contributions of their converts. However this may be, the treasures accumulated, through the credulous piety of the faithful, became an object of the avarice of priests, and begat discord among them. Each one wishing to govern, and have the disposal of the riches of the community. Hence the cabals and factions which we find growing up with the church of God. The priests were always first to wander from the principles of their religion. Their own ambition and avarice always contradict the disinterested maxims they teach to others.

So long as the Christian religion was much depressed and persecuted, discordant Bishops and priests combated in secret, and the noise of their quarrels did not spread far abroad. But when Constantine wished to secure to himself a party, the obscurity of which had favoured its increase, until now become very numerous, the face of every thing in the church was changed. Christian leaders, transformed to courtiers, and seduced by authority, fought openly. They engaged sovereigns in their quarrels, and persecuted their rivals. Laden by degrees with riches

---

[37] Saint Jerome highly disapproved the distinctions of bishops and priests or curates. He pretends, that priests and bishops were, according to St. Paul, the same thing, before, says he, by the instigation of the devil, there were destinations in religion. At this day, bishops, who do nothing, enjoy great revenues; innumerable curates, who labour, are dying with hunger.

and honours, they would no longer be recognized, as the successors of the poor and humble Apostles, sent by Christ to preach his doctrine. They became princes, and, supported by the strongest arms, opinions, they found themselves able to give laws to nations, and put the world in confusion.

Under Constantine, the Pontificate had been by a shameful imprudence separated from the empire. The Emperors soon found they had cause to repent this oversight. The Bishop of Rome, that former mistress of the world, whose name still sounded awful in the ears of nations, knew how to make a skilful advantage of the troubles of the empire, invaded by barbarians, and the weakness of Emperors, too remote to watch over his conduct. By dint of plots and intrigues, the Roman pontiff at length seated himself on the throne of the Caesars. It was for him that Emilius and Scipio had fought. He was, in fine, looked upon in the west, as the monarch of the Church, the universal bishop, the vicar of Jesus Christ upon earth, and the infallible organ of God. Although these haughty titles were rejected in the East, the Roman pontiff reigned, without contest, in the greater part of the Christian world. He was a God upon earth; through the imbecility of kings, he became arbiter of their destinies, and founded a theocracy or divine government, of which himself was chief, and they were his lieutenants. When they had the audacity to become disobedient to him, he dethroned them, or excited their subjects to rebellion. In a word, his spiritual arms were, through a long succession of ages, stronger than the temporal ones of his opponents. Nations had the stupidity to obey him, and the distribution of Crowns was in his power. To secure his dominion over princes, he sowed divisions among them; and his empire would still retain its extent and vigour, if a gradual increase of knowledge, had not, in spite of religious opposition, made its way among mankind, and kings, acting inconsistently with their religion, listened to ambition rather than duty. If the ministers of the Church have received their power from Christ himself, to resist these his representatives is, in fact, to revolt against him. Kings, as well as subjects, cannot throw off allegiance to God without a crime. The spiritual authority proceeding from God, must, of right, have jurisdiction over temporal authority proceeding from man. A prince, who is a true Christian, must become a servant of the church, and, at best, the first slave of the clergy.

Let us not, then, be surprised, that, in the ages of ignorance, priests, being most readily obeyed by people, more attached to heavenly than earthly interests, were more powerful than kings. Among superstitious nations, the pretended voice of God and his interests is more listened to, than that of duty, justice, and reason. A good Christian, piously submissive to the Church, must be blind and unreasonable, whenever the church commands him to be so. The power that has a right to render us absurd, has the right to render us criminal.

Besides, those that derive their power from God, can be subject to no other power. Thus, the independence of the Christian clergy, is founded upon the principles of their religion. Of this circumstance, they have taken care to profit, and impressed with this idea, they, after being enriched by the generosity of kings and people, have always proved ungrateful to the true sources of their own opulence and privileges. What had been given this body, through surprise or impudence, it was found impossible to recover from their hands. They foresaw, that future generations, breaking loose from the fetters of prejudice, might tear from them the donations they had gained by the extortions of terror, and the evils of imposture. They, therefore, persuaded mankind that they held from God alone, what had been given them by their fellow mortals: and by a miracle of credulity, they were believed on their word.

Thus the interests of the clergy became separated from those of society. Men devoted to God, and chosen to be his ministers, were no longer confounded with the profane. Laws and civil tribunals renounced all power over them. They could be judged only by members of their own body. Hence the greatest excesses were often committed by them with impunity; and their persons, at the disposal of God alone, were sacred and inviolable. Their possessions, although they contributed nothing to public charges. or, at least, no more than they pleased, were defended and enlarged by fanatic sovereigns, who hoped thereby to conciliate the favour of Heaven. In fact, those reverend wolves in shepherds clothing, under pretence of feeding with instruction, devoured with avarice, and, secure in their disguise, fattened on the blood of their flocks, unpunished and unsuspected. From their instructions for eighteen hundred years past, what advantages have nations derived? Have these infallible men found it possible to agree among themselves, on the most essential points of a religion, revealed by God himself? Strange, indeed, is that revelation, which needs continual commentaries, and interpretations. What must be thought of these divine writings, which every sect understands so differently? Those who are incessantly fed with the gospel, do not understand these matters better, nor are they more virtuous than others. They are commanded to obey the Church, and the Church is never at accord with itself. She is eternally busied, in reforming, explaining, pulling down, and building up her holy doctrines. Her ministers have, at will, created new doctrines unknown to Christ and the Apostles. Every age has brought forth new mysteries, new ceremonies, and new articles of faith. Notwithstanding the inspirations of the Holy Ghost, this religion has never attained to that clearness, simplicity, and consistency, which are the only indubitable proofs of a good system. Neither councils, nor canons, nor the mass of decrees and laws, which form the code of the Church, have ever yet been able to fix the objects of her belief.

Were a sensible heathen desirous of embracing Christianity, he would be, at the first step, thrown into perplexity, at the sight of the numerous variety of sects, each of which, pretends to conform precisely to the word of God, and travel in the only sure road to salvation. When he finds that these different sects regard each other with horror; that they all deal out damnation to all, whose opinions differ from their own; that they all unite their efforts to banish peace from society; that always, when power is in their hands, they persecute and inflict the most refined cruelties on each other, for which shall he determine? For, let us not be deceived-- Christians, not satisfied with enforcing by violence, an exterior submission to the ceremonies of their religion, have invented an art unknown to heathen superstitions, that of tormenting the conscience, and exercising a tyranny over the mind itself. The zeal of the ministers of the Church is not limited to exteriors; they steal into the foldings of the heart, and insolently violate the most secret sanctuaries of thought.[38] And for this sacrilege, their justification is a pretended interest in the salvation of souls.

Such are the effects which necessarily result from the principles of a religion, which teaches mankind that involuntary error is a crime that merits the wrath of God. It is an consequence of such ideas, that in certain countries, priests, with the permission of the civil governments, pretend to a commission for maintaining the faith in its purity. Judges in their own cause, they condemn to the flames all whose opinions appear to them dangerous.[39] Served by innumerable spies, they watch the minutest actions of the people, and inhumanly sacrifice all that have the misfortune to give them the smallest umbrage. To excite suspicions in their minds, is to rush upon inevitable destruction. Such are the blessings which the Holy Inquisition, all mild and gentle, pours upon mankind.

Such are the principles of this sanguinary tribunal which perpetuates the ignorance and infatuation of the people wherever the false policy or governments permits its horrors to be exercised.

---

[38] Spoken of the Romish Clergy.

[39] Civil tribunals, when they are just, have a maxim to look for every thing that can contribute to the defence of the accused. In the Inquisition a method directly opposite has been adopted. The accused is neither told the cause of his detention nor confronted with his accuser. He is ignorant of his crime, yet he commanded to confess. Such are the maxims of Christian priests. The Inquisition, however, condemns nobody to die. Priests cannot themselves shed blood. That function is reserved for the Secular arm; and they have even the effrontery to intercede for criminals, sure, however, of not being heard. Indeed, it is probable, they would make no small clamour, should the magistrate take them at their word. This conduct becomes men in whom Almighty interest stifles humanity, sincerely, and modesty.

The disputes between Christian priests have been sources of animosity, hatred, and heresy. We find these to have existed from the infancy of the church. A religion founded on wonders, fables, and obscure oracles, could only be a fruitful source of quarrels. Priests attended to ridiculous doctrines instead of useful knowledge; and when they should have studied true morality, and taught mankind their real duties, they only strove to gain adherents. They busied themselves in useless speculations in a barbarous and enigmatical science, which, under the pompous title of the science of God, or theology, excited in the vulgar a reverential awe. They invented a system, bigoted, presumptuous, ridiculous, and as incomprehensible as the God whom they affected to worship. Hence arose disputes on disputes, concerning puerile subtleties, odious questions, and arbitrary opinions, which far from being useful, only served to poison the peace of society. In these bickerings we find profound geniuses busied; and we are forced to reject the prostitution of talents worthy a better cause. The vulgar, ever fond of riot, entered into quarrels they could not understand. Princes undertook the defence of the priests they wished to favour, and orthodoxy was decided by the longest sword. Their assistance the church never hesitated to receive in time of danger; for on such occasion the church relies rather on human assistance, than the promise of God, who declared that the sceptre of the wicked should not rest upon the lot of the righteous. The heroes, found in the annals of the church, have been obstinate fanatics, factious rebels, or furious persecutors. They were monsters of madness, faction, and cruelty. The world, in the days of our ancestors, was depopulated in defence of extravagancies which excite laughter in a posterity, not indeed much wiser than they were.

In almost all ages complaints have been made of abuses in the church, and reformation has been talked of. Notwithstanding this pretended reform, in the head, and in the members of the church, it has always been corrupted. Avaricious, turbulent, and seditious priests have made nations to groan under the weight of their vices, while princes were too week to reclaim them to reason.

The divisions and quarrels which took place among those ecclesiastical tyrants did indeed at length diminish the weight of the yoke they had imposed on kings and nations. The empire of the Roman pontiff which endured many ages, was at last shaken by irritated enthusiasts, and rebellious subjects, who presumed to examine the rights of this formidable despot. Some princes, weary of their slavery and poverty, readily embraced opinions which would authorise them to enrich themselves with the spoils of the clergy. Thus the unity of the church was destroyed, sects were multiplied, and each fought for the defence of his own system.

These founders of these new sects were treated by the Roman pontiff as innovators, heretics, and blasphemers. They, it is true, renounced some of their old opinions; but content with having made a few steps towards reason, they dared not to shake off entirely the yoke of superstition. They continued to respect the sacred writ of the Christian, which they still looked upon as the only faithful guide. Upon them they pretended to found all their opinions. In fine, these books, in which every man may find what he pleases, as they became more common from time to time, produced new sects. Men were lost in a dark labyrinth, where each one groped his way in error, and yet judged all but himself to be wrong.

The leaders of these sects, the pretended reformers of the church, gained but a glimpse at the truth, and attended to nothing but minutiae. They continued to respect the sacred oracles of the Christians, and believe in their cruel and capricious God. They admitted their extravagant mythology, and most of their unreasonable doctrines. In fine, although they rejected some mysteries that were incomprehensible, they admitted others not less so. Let us not be surprised, therefore, that, notwithstanding these reforms, fanaticism, controversy, persecution, and war, continued to rage throughout Europe. The reveries of innovators only served to plunge nations into new misfortunes. Blood continued to stream, and people grew neither more reasonable nor more happy. Priests of all sects have ever wished to govern mankind and impose on them their decisions as infallible and sacred. They were always persecutors when in power, involved nations in their fury, and shook the world by their fatal opinions. The spirit of intolerance and persecution will ever be the essence of every sect founded on the Bible. A mild and humane religion can never belong to a partial and cruel God, whom the opinions of men can fill with wrath. Wherever Christian sects exist, priests will exercise a power which may prove fatal to the state, and bodies of fanatical enthusiasts will be formed, always ready to rush to slaughter, when their spiritual guides cry, the church or the cause of God is in danger.

Thus, in Christian countries, we see the temporal power servilely submissive to the clergy, executing their commands, exterminating their enemies, and supporting their rights, riches, and immunities. In almost all nations where the church prevails, the most idle, useless, seditious, and dangerous men are most liberally honoured and rewarded. Superstition thinks she can never do enough for the ministers of her gods. These sentiments are the same in all sects.[40] Priests every where endeavour to instil them into kings, and to make policy bend to religion, in doing which they often oppose the best institutions. They in all places aim at the superintendance of education, and they fill their adherents with their fatal prejudices from their infancy.

It is, however, in places that remained subject to the Roman pontiff, that the clergy have wallowed in the greatest profusion of riches and power. Credulity has even enlisted kings among their subjects, and debased them into mere executioners of their will. They were in readiness to unsheath the sword whenever the priest commanded it. The monarchs of the Roman sect, blinder than all others, had an unbounded confidence in the clergy of their church that generally rendered them mere tools of that body. This sect, by means of furious intolerance and atrocious persecutions, became more numerous than any other one; and their turbulent and cruel temper has justly rendered them odious to the most reasonable, that is to say, least Christian nations.

---

[40] Except the Quakers.

The Romish system was, in fact, invented to throw all the power into the hands of the clergy. Its priests have had the address to identify themselves with God. Their cause was always his; their glory became the glory of God. Their decisions were divine oracles; their possessions appertained to the kingdom of heaven. Their pride, avarice, and cruelty, were rendered lawful, because they were never actuated by other motives than the interest of their heavenly master. In this sect, the priest saw his king at his feet, humbly confessing his sins, and beseeching the holy man that he might be reconciled to his God. Seldom was the priest known to render this sacred minister subservient to the good of mankind. He thought not of reproaching monarchs with the abuse of their power, the misery of their subjects, and the tears of the oppressed. Too timid, or too much of a courtier to thunder truth in their ears, he mentioned not to them the insupportable oppressions, the galling tyranny, and useless wars under which their subjects groaned. But such objects never interest the church, which might indeed be of some utility, if its influence were exercised in bridling the excesses of superstitious tyrants. The terrors of the other world would not be unpardonable falsehoods, could they make the herd of wicked kings to tremble. This, however, has not been the object of the ministers of religion. They never stickled for the interest of mankind. They always burned incense at the altar of tyranny, looked upon its crimes with indulgence, and devised for them easy means of expiation. Tyrants were sure of the pardon and favour of heaven, if they entered warmly into the quarrels of the clergy. Thus, among the Catholics, priests governed kings, and consequently all their subjects. Superstition and despotism formed an internal alliance, and united their efforts, to plunge mankind into slavery and wretchedness. Priests frightened nations with religious terror, that they might he preyed upon by their sovereigns at leisure; and, in return, those sovereigns loaded the priests with opulence and power, and undertook, from time to time, to exterminate their enemies.

What shall we say of those subtle geniuses which Christians call casuists, those pretended moralists who have computed the number of sins against God which a man can commit without risking his salvation? These men of profound wisdom have enriched Christian morality with a ridiculous *tarif* of sins; they know precisely the degree of wrath which each excites in the breast of the Almighty. True morality has but one criterion for judging the sins of man; the greatest are those that injure society most. The conduct which injures ourselves in imprudent and unreasonable. That which injures others is unjust and criminal.

Every thing, even to idleness itself, is rewarded in Christian priests. Multitudes of these drones are maintained in ease and affluence, while, instead of serving society, they only prey upon it. They are paid with profusion for useless prayers which they make with negligence. And while monks and lazy priests, those bloodsuckers of society, wallow in an abundance shameful to the states by whom they are tolerated, the man of talents, the man of science, and the brave soldier are suffered to languish in indigence, and poorly exist on the mere necessaries of life.

In a word, Christianity makes nations accomplices in all the evils which are heaped upon them by the Clergy. Neither the uselessness of their prayers demonstrated by the experience of so many ages, the bloody effects of their fatal controversies, nor even their licentious excesses, have yet been sufficient to convince mankind how shamefully they are duped by that infallible Church, to the existence of which they have had the simplicity to believe, their salvation attached.

CHAP. XVI

CONCLUSION.

ALL which has hitherto been said, demonstrates, in the clearest manner, that the Christian religion is contrary to true policy, and the welfare of mankind. It can be advantageous only to ignorant and vicious princes, who are desirous to reign over slaves, and who, in order to strip and tyrannize over them with impunity, form a league with the priesthood, whose function it has ever been to deceive in the name of heaven. But such imprudent princes should remember, that, in order to succeed in their projects, they must themselves become the staves of the priesthood, who (should the former fail in due submission, or refuse to be subservient to their passions) will infallibly turn their sacred arms against their royal heads.

We have seen, above, that the Christian religion is not, on account of its fanatic virtues, blind zeal, and pretended perfections, the less injurious to sound morality, right reason, the happiness of individuals, and domestic harmony. It is easy to perceive that a Christian, who proposes to himself as a model, a gloomy and suffering God, must take pains to afflict and render himself wretched, if this world be only a passage, if this life be only a pilgrimage, it must be ridiculous for a man to attach himself to any thing here below. If his God be offended with either the actions or opinions of his fellow-creatures, he must do every thing in his power to punish them with severity, or be wanting in zeal seed affection to his God. A good Christian must fly the world, or become a torment to himself and others.

These reflections are sufficient to answer those who pretend that the Christian religion is the foundation of true policy and morality, and that where it is not professed there can be neither good men nor good citizens. The converse of this proposition is undoubtedly much truer; for we may assert, that a perfect Christian, who conforms to all the principles of his religion, who faithfully imitates the divine men proposed to him as a model, and practices their austerities in solitude, or carries their fanatic enthusiasm and bigotry into society, must be either useless to mankind, or a troublesome and dangerous citizen. [41]

Were we to believe the advocates of the Christian religion, it would appear, that no morality can exist where this religion is not established. Yet we may perceive, at a single glance, that there are virtues in every corner of the earth. No political society could exist without them. Among the Chinese, the Indians, and the Mahometans, there are, undoubtedly, good citizens, tender fathers, affectionate husbands, and dutiful children. And good people there, as well as with us, would be more numerous if they were governed by a wise policy, which, instead of causing children to be taught a senseless religion, should give them equitable laws, teach them a pure morality uncontaminated with fanaticism, deter them from vice by suitable punishments, and invite them to the practice of virtue by proper rewards.

In truth, it seems (I repeat it) that religion has been invented to relieve governments from the care of being just, and reigning by equitable laws. Religion is the art of inspiring mankind with an enthusiasm. which is designed to divert their attention from the evils with which they are overwhelmed by those who govern them. By means of the invisible powers with which they are threatened, they are forced to suffer in silence the miseries with which they are afflicted by visible ones. They are taught to hope that, if they consent to become miserable in this world, they will for that reason be happy in the next.

Thus religion has become the most powerful support of a shameful and iniquitous policy, which holds it necessary to deceive mankind, that they may the more easily be governed. Far

---

[41] The clergy incessantly cry out against unbelievers and philosophers, whom they style dangerous subjects. Yet, if we open history, we do not find that philosophers are those who have embroiled states and empires; but that such events have generally been produced by the religious. The Dominican, who poisoned the emperor Henry XI. James Clement and Ravaillac, were not unbelievers. They were not philosophers, but fanatic Christians, who led Charles I. to the scaffold. It was the minister Gomare, and not Spinosa, who set Holland on fire, &c. &c. &c.

from enlightened and virtuous governments be resources so base! Let them learn their true interests, and know that these cannot be separated from that of the people. Let them know that no state can be truly potent, except the citizens who compose it be courageous, active, industrious, virtuous, and attached to their government. Let governments know, that the attachment of their constituents can have no other foundation than the happiness which the former procures the latter. If governments were penetrated with these important truths, they would need the aid of neither religion nor priests. Let them be just and equitable--let them be careful to reward talents and virtue, to discourage inutility and punish vice, and their states will soon he filled with worthy and sensible citizens, who will feel it their own interest to serve and defend their country, and support the government which is the instrument of their felicity. They will do their duties, without the influence of revelation, or mysteries of paradise or hell.

Morality will be preached in vain if it is not supported by the example of influential characters. It belongs to magistrates to teach morality, by *practising* it, by inciting to virtue and repressing vice in every form. Their power is weakened the moment they suffer a power to arise in the state, whose influence is exerted to render morality subservient to superstition and fanaticism. In states where education is entrusted to a fanatic enthusiastic clergy, we find citizens overwhelmed with superstition, and destitute of every virtue, except a blind faith, a ferocious zeal, a ridiculous submission to puerile ceremonies, and, in one word, fantastic notions, which never render them better men. Notwithstanding the happy influences attributed to the Christian religion, do we find more virtues in those who profess it, than in those who are strangers to it? Are the men, redeemed by the blood of even a Deity, more honest than others? Among Christians, impressed with their religion, one would imagine, we should search in vain for rapine, fornication, adultery, and oppression. Among the orthodox courtiers, who surround Christian thrones, do we see intrigues, calumny, or perfidy?

Among the clergy, who announce to others such redoubtable dogmas, and such terrible chastisements, do we find crimes that shun the day, and every species of iniquity? All these men are Christians, who, unbridled by their religion, continually violate the plainest duties of morality, and knowingly offend a God, whom they are conscious of having irritated. Yet they flatter themselves that they shall be able, by a tardy repentance at death, to appease that divine justice which they have insulted during the whole course of their lives.

In the mean time, we shall not deny, that the Christian religion sometimes proves a restraint to timorous minds, which are incapable of that fanaticism, and destitute of that destructive energy, which leads to the commission of great crimes. But such minds would have been honest and harmless without this restraint. The fear of rendering themselves odious to mankind, of incurring contempt, and losing their reputation, would have been a chain of equal strength, on the actions of such men. Those who are so blind as to tread these considerations under foot, would never be deterred from it by the menaces of religion.

Every man, who has received a proper education, experiences within himself a painful sentiment of mingled shame and fear, whenever he soils himself with the guilt of a dishonest action. He even condemns himself frequently, with greater severity than others do. He dreads, and shuns the eyes of his fellow-creatures; he even wishes to fly from himself. This is what constitutes remorse.

In a word, Christianity puts no restraint upon the passions of mankind, which might not be more efficaciously applied to them by reason, education, and sound morality. If the wicked were sure of being punished, as often as they think of committing dishonest actions, they would be forced to desist. In a society well constituted, contempt will always follow vice, and crimes will produce punishment. Education, guided only by the good of society, ought ever to teach mankind to esteem themselves, to dread the contempt of others, and fear infamy more than death itself. But this kind of morality can never be consistent with a religion which commands men to despise themselves, avoid the esteem of others, and attempt to please only a God, whose conduct is inexplicable.

In fine, if the Christian religion be, as is pretended, a restraint to the crimes of men, if it produces salutary effects on some individuals; can these advantages, so rare, so weak and doubtful, be compared with the evident and immense evils which this religion has produced on the earth? Can some few trifling crimes prevented, some conversions useless to society, some steril and tardy repentances, enter into the balance against the continual dissensions, bloody wars, horrid massacres, persecutions, and cruelties, of which the Christian religion has been a continual cause and pretext? For one secret sinful thought suppressed by it, there are even whole nations armed for reciprocal destruction; the hearts of millions of fanatics are inflamed; families and states are plunged into confusion; and the earth is bedewed with tears and blood.[42] After this, let common sense decide the magnitude of the advantages which mankind derive from the glad tidings which Christians pretend to have received from their God.

Many honest people, although not ignorant of the ills produced among mankind by this religion, nevertheless consider it a necessary evil, and think it dangerous to attempt to uproot it. Mankind, say they, are naturally superstitious; they must be amused with chimeras, and become outrageous when deprived of them. But, I answer, mankind are superstitious only because, in infancy, every thing contributes to render them so. He is led to expect his happiness from chimeras, because he is forbidden to seek for it from realities.

In fine, it is for philosophers and for magistrates to conduct mankind back to reason. The former will obtain the confidence and love of the latter, when they endeavour to promote the public good. Undeceived themselves, they may undeceive others by degrees. Governments will prevent superstition from doing harm,

---

[42] Witness, even in this enlightened age, the Holy Crusade against France, for the purpose of restoring the Christian religion.

when they despise it and stand aloof from its ridiculous disputes. When they tolerate all sects, and side with none, those sects, after quarrelling awhile, will drop their masks, and become contemptible even to themselves. Superstition falls beneath its own weight when, freedom of conscience being restored to mankind, reason is at liberty to attack their follies. True toleration and freedom of thought are the most proper instruments for the destruction of religious fanaticism. Imposture is in nature timid, and when she finds herself confronted with truth, her arms fall from her hands.

If a criminal and undiscerning policy has, hitherto, in almost all parts of the earth, had recourse to the aid of religion, to enslave mankind and render them miserable, let a virtuous and more enlightened policy hereafter destroy it by little and little to render them happy. If education has hitherto formed enthusiasts and fanatics, let it be hereafter calculated to form good citizens. If a morality founded on miracles, and looking to futurity, has been unable to restrain the passions of mankind, let a morality established upon their present and real wants demonstrate that, in a well constituted society, happiness is always the reward of virtue: shame, contempt, and punishment the companions of vice, and the wages of sin.

If error be an evil, to it let truth be opposed. If enthusiasm produce disorders in society; let it be suppressed. Let us leave to Asia a religion begotten by the ardent imaginations of the orientals. Let our milder climates be more reasonable, more free, and more happy. Let us make them the residence of honesty, activity, industry, social affections, and exalted minds. May not reason be permitted to hope, that she shall one day reassume the power so long usurped from her by error, illusion, and deceit? When will nations renounce chimerical hopes, to contemplate their true interests? Will they never shake off the yokes of those hypocritical tyrants, who are interested only in the errors of mankind? Let us hope it. Truth must at last triumph over falsehood.-- Mankind, fatigued with their own credulity, will return to her arms.--Reason will break their chains.--Reason, which was created to reign, with undivided empire over all intelligent beings.

AMEN.

www.ingramcontent.com/pod-product-compliance
Lightning Source LLC
Chambersburg PA
CBHW071731090426
42738CB00011B/2454